THE HAMLYN LECTURES

FOURTH SERIES

ENGLISH LAW AND THE MORAL LAW

AUSTRALIA

The Law Book Co. of Australasia Pty Ltd.
Sydney : Melbourne : Brisbane

CANADA AND U.S.A.

The Carswell Company Ltd.
Toronto

INDIA

N. M. Tripathi Ltd.
Bombay

NEW ZEALAND

Legal Publications Ltd.
Wellington

PAKISTAN

Pakistan Law House
Karachi

ENGLISH LAW AND
THE MORAL LAW

BY

A. L. GOODHART,

K.B.E., Q.C., F.B.A.,

Master of University College, Oxford

Published under the auspices of
THE HAMLYN TRUST

LONDON
STEVENS & SONS LIMITED
1953

*First published in 1953 by
Stevens & Sons Limited
of 119 & 120 Chancery Lane
London – Law Publishers
and printed in Great Britain
by The Eastern Press Ltd.
of London and Reading*

CONTENTS

HAMLYN LECTURERS

THE HAMLYN TRUST

THE Hamlyn Trust came into existence under the will
of the late Miss Emma Warburton Hamlyn, of
Torquay, who died in 1941 aged 80. She came of
an old and well-known Devon family. Her father,
William Bussell Hamlyn, practised in Torquay as a
solicitor for many years. She was a woman of
dominant character, intelligent and cultured, well
versed in literature, music, and art, and a lover of
her country. She inherited a taste for law, and
studied the subject. She travelled frequently on the
Continent and about the Mediterranean and gathered
impressions of comparative jurisprudence and
ethnology.

Miss Hamlyn bequeathed the residue of her estate
in terms which were thought vague. The matter was
taken to the Chancery Division of the High Court,
which on November 29, 1948, approved a Scheme for
the administration of the Trust. Paragraph 3 of the
Scheme is as follows : —

"The object of this charity is the furtherance
by lectures or otherwise among the Common
People of the United Kingdom of Great Britain
and Northern Ireland of the knowledge of the
Comparative Jurisprudence and the Ethnology of
the Chief European Countries, including the
United Kingdom, and the circumstances of the
growth of such Jurisprudence to the intent that
the Common People of the United Kingdom may
realise the privileges which in law and custom

they enjoy in comparison with other European Peoples and realising and appreciating such privileges may recognise the responsibilities and obligations attaching to them."

The Trustees under the Scheme number nine, *viz.*:

(*a*) Mr. S. K. COLERIDGE,   Executors of
     Mr. J. R. WARBURTON   Miss Hamlyn's Will.

(*b*) Representatives of the Universities of London, Wales, Leeds, Glasgow and Belfast, *viz.*:

    Professor G. W. KEETON,
    Professor D. J. Ll. DAVIES,
    Professor B. A. WORTLEY,
    Glasgow (vacant),
    Professor E. ASHBY.

(*c*) The Principal of the University College of the South-West, *ex officio* (vacant).

(*d*) Dr. John MURRAY (*co-opted*).

The Trustees decided to organise courses of lectures of high interest and quality by persons of eminence under the auspices of co-operating Universities with a view to the lectures being made available in book form to a wide public.

The fourth series of four lectures was delivered by Dr. Goodhart, in the University of Manchester, in November, 1952.

JOHN MURRAY,
Chairman of the Trustees.

October, 1953.

PREFACE

SOME years ago when I called on a distinguished Oxford philosopher, I heard him say in a worried voice to one of his pupils, "I am not at all happy about pleasure." When I delivered the Hamlyn Lectures at the University of Manchester last November I was not at all happy concerning the relation between *sanction* and *law*. In defining law as a rule of human conduct which is recognised as being obligatory I rejected the view that the sanction is an essential element in law. It did not seem to me that it was possible to explain constitutional law, international law, religious law, or moral law in terms of a threatened evil. On the other hand, it is clear that in almost every legal system there are some men who may fail to recognise any obligation to obey the law, and who can be controlled only by the imposition of a sanction. How then can law be defined solely in terms of obligation as this would seem to leave out this small but not unimportant group? The answer, which I am suggesting in these lectures, is that in those instances the recognition which we are talking about is the recognition on the part of the judges that the rule is obligatory. The sanction is applied because they recognise that the rule is obligatory: the rule is not obligatory because there is a sanction. If this were not true then it would be impossible to distinguish between law and arbitrary command. After I had reached this conclusion Professor Hart, my successor

ix

as Professor of Jurisprudence at Oxford, called my
attention to Professor Axel Hägerström's *Inquiries
into the Nature of Law and Morals*, recently translated
by Professor C. D. Broad, which supports the views I
have expressed here. He emphasises (p. 210) that
there is a fundamental difference " between the fact
that an action is commanded and its being a duty."
This duty cannot be explained in terms of a sanction.

Having reached the conclusion that law depends on
the recognition of an obligation it has been possible
for me to suggest that the moral law has played a
more important role in relation to State law than
many legal philosophers have been prepared to admit.
In these lectures I have attempted to show that there
is not a single branch of English law which does not,
to a considerable degree, find both its origin and its
force in the moral convictions of the English people.

The delay in finally preparing my lectures for the
press has given me the welcome opportunity of
expressing to the University of Manchester, and
especially to its faculty of law, my gratitude for the
cordial way in which I was received by them. I also
wish to thank Professor Hart and Mr. Peter Strawson,
both Fellows of my College, for their valuable
criticisms. I hasten to add that they cannot be held
responsible for any of the views which I have expressed
in these lectures.

A. L. GOODHART.

September, 1953.

THE NATURE OF LAW
AND OF MORALS

1

THE NATURE OF LAW AND OF MORALS

THE purpose of the Hamlyn Lectures is to bring to the attention of the people of Great Britain and Northern Ireland the privileges which they enjoy under the law, so that they may recognise the responsibilities and obligations which are attached to these privileges. The recognition by the people of this island that the law under which they live is one of their greatest heritages has, as I hope to show in these lectures, always been one of the foundations on which the strength of the State is based, but never has this recognition been more important than at the present time when both the State and the law are under attack by those who wish to destroy our existing civilisation. The Roman citizen's proudest boast was that he lived under the Roman law, and today the men and women living in these islands can make the same claim for the common law. I think that it is true to say that the basic conflict between the Western idea of life and that which has been dominant in the totalitarian States is a juridical one. There are, of course, radical differences in their conceptions concerning religion, systems of government and the economic structure, but in none of them is the difference more fundamental than in the interpretation of law. It is not true to say that the totalitarian States

have not got systems of law, but their law is regarded
essentially as an expression of power by those in
control: it safeguards " arrangements agreeable and
advantageous to the dominant [proletarian] class." [1]
In England no such doctrine has ever been accepted.
It is refuted in the most solemn Act of State under
the British constitution. In administering the Corona-
tion Oath the Archbishop of Canterbury asks the
Queen whether she will solemnly promise and swear to
govern the Peoples of the United Kingdom of Great
Britain and Northern Ireland and of the Empire
" according to their respective laws and customs," and
" Will you to your power cause Law and Justice, in
Mercy, to be executed in all your judgments? " To
this the Queen replies: " I solemnly promise so to do."
This ancient oath expresses in dramatic form the basic
principle that those who rule in Great Britain are
bound by the laws and customs of the country, and
that these laws and customs are not an expression of
sovereign will. It is because England has been a
nation founded on law for a longer period than any
other State in the history of the world, and because
it is still pre-eminent in this respect that it is so
important for us to realise the part that law plays in
the life of this country. Law and freedom are here
so closely bound together that we cannot think of the
one without the other; it is for this reason that the
English polity has for centuries been regarded as a

[1] S. A. Golunskii and M. S. Strogovich, " Theory of the State
and Law " in *Soviet Legal Philosophy*, Harvard University
Press, 1951, at p. 370.

model by all those who seek liberty throughout the world.[2]

I am not suggesting that law is identical with freedom or justice. Law is merely a piece of machinery and can be used either for or against liberty. Law is not necessarily either reasonable or moral. When St. Thomas Aquinas defined law as " an ordinance of reason made for the common good by the public personage who has charge of the community " [3] he was, I believe, speaking of an ideal law, for he must have recognised that there were many legal provisions which could not be regarded as necessarily reasonable. Law ought to be based on reason, it ought to protect liberty, and it ought to be in accord with the moral law, but these ideals are not a necessary part of our conception of law.[4]

On the other hand, it is, I believe, equally wrong to suggest that law is necessarily an instrument used by those in power to enforce their will on those who

[2] It is hardly necessary to point out that the closest bond between Great Britain and the United States is found in the common law. The American colonists in 1775 claimed that George III and his Parliament were denying to them the common law rights to which they were entitled.

[3] *Summa Theologica*, 1a–2ae. XC. 4.

[4] Professor Rheinstein in his article " The Relation of Morals to Law " (1952) *Journal of Public Law*, Emory University, Georgia, 287–300, has said (p. 292): " Among such efforts to define law as containing essentially some ethical value, two groups may be distinguished, *viz.*: first, definitions containing some concrete ethical value, such as liberty (Kant, Stammler, recently also Bodenheimer) or reason (St. Thomas, rationalists); and second, definitions containing some formal element to be filled with varying ethical contents, such as the proletarian class interest (Communists), the interest of the national or racial community (National-Socialists), culture (Gurvitch), reciprocity (Malinowski), or ethical-imperative co-ordination (Timasheff).

are under their control. Plato in *The Republic* [5] makes Thrasymachus, the Sophist philosopher, define law as " the interest of the strongest party." More than two thousand years later the Soviet Decree of December 12, 1919,[6] defined law as " a set of rules for social relationships, which corresponds to the interests of the dominant class and is safeguarded by the organised force of that class." The Russian legal philosopher Pashukanis therefore argued that with the final establishment of the proletarian system all law would disappear. He said [7]: " The dying out of the categories of bourgeois law will in these conditions signify the dying out of law in general: that is to say, the gradual disappearance of the juridic element in human relations." Unfortunately for Pashukanis, who himself disappeared into the unknown in 1938, this view has been rejected by the more recent Soviet rulers who have found that it is impossible for a State to function without a system of law. In a famous address entitled " Fundamental Tasks of Soviet Law," which heralded the destruction of Pashukanis, Mr. A. Y. Vyshinsky said [8]:

" In speaking of the impossibility of constructing a theory of law, these persons [Pashukanis and Stucka] were driven to assert that it was impossible to construct even a system of Soviet socialist law. It is clear that—starting from these two basic

---

[5] Chap. 3, I. 337.
[6] Cited by Professor John Hazard in introduction to *Soviet Legal Philosophy*, p. xxiii.
[7] E. B. Pashukanis, " Theory of Law and Marxism," in *Soviet Legal Philosophy*, p. 122.
[8] *Soviet Legal Philosophy*, p. 331.

wrecker designs of theirs—they could furnish neither a theory nor a system of Soviet socialist law. Traitors and betrayers as they were, they were not merely unable to provide a working out of these most important tasks confronting the science of Soviet law—they did not even wish to do so. This gang of thieves, betrayers and traitors crept into certain of our institutes and made a mockery of our science."

Mr. Vyshinsky was here expressing in stronger terms than are usually used in philosophic discussions in this country the view that law is essential in every State. This is undoubtedly true, but what is of equal importance is the purpose of the law which is under consideration. If this is directed to the achievement of freedom and justice then it can be described as beneficent: if on the other hand it is used as a tool by an autocratic government then it assumes the character of those who find in it an instrument by which they can control those under their absolute power. The quality of the law therefore depends on the purpose to which it is directed.

In these lectures I shall not ascribe unlimited virtue to the English law. From time to time certain provisions of that law have been directed to ends of which we today cannot approve, and there are undoubtedly parts of the present law which are subject to criticism. It is, however, true to say that in England the major purposes of the law have been to achieve self-government, individual freedom, and justice between men. We find this expressed in our phrase the Common Law. It is a law which is common to all of

us, and which is based on our common will. The three
major purposes which I have stated all contain a moral
quality because without freedom a man is not capable
of full development as a human being, and without
justice law is nothing more than a system of arbitrary
rules. There is in England, therefore, a close bond
between law and morals and it is impossible to understand the nature of English law unless we also
recognise the various moral ideas which it represents.
Before I attempt to deal with this essential link
between law and morals in English law it will be
necessary for me to define what I mean by law, and
what I mean by morals.

LAW IN GENERAL

I shall begin by saying some words about law in
general, because it is only if we understand what we
mean by the nature of law in this sense that we can
adequately discern the essential elements of our
English law. In its most general sense the word *law*
covers any uniformity of conduct, including even the
conduct of inanimate things.[9] Thus we talk of the law
of gravity to express the fact that an apple when
dropped will fall to the ground. This uniformity
applies also to animate beings when we describe the
physical results which follow on their conduct.

Such a definition of law as a mere expression of
uniformity is obviously not adequate when we turn to

---

[9] Sir William Blackstone in his *Commentaries* (1765), Introduction, s. 2, said: '' Law in its most general and comprehensive
sense signifies a rule of action; and is applied indiscriminately
to all kinds of action, whether animate or inanimate, rational
or irrational.''

law in social life. When we speak of religious law, moral law or State law we are not merely referring to uniformity of conduct; we are concerned with rules which are established for the purpose of achieving uniformity. Perhaps the distinction between the use of the word *law* in the physical and the social sciences has been best defined by saying that in the physical sciences we have a *description* of conduct, while in the social sciences we have a *prescription* for conduct. I think that it is correct to say that all legal philosophers are agreed that the word *law* should be used by them in the latter sense, but where they are in fundamental disagreement is in their conclusions concerning the nature of the prescription. It is obvious that an answer to this question is of the greatest importance because if we accept the view that the essential element in law is force then we shall regard law merely as an expression of power, while if we regard the essential element of law as consent then we will place all our emphasis on reason.[10] I shall suggest that the answer is a far more complicated one than either of these, and that the compulsive nature of law, which distinguishes it from all other rules, may owe its existence to many different causes.

[10] In his delightful article on " Language and the Law " (1945) 61 *Law Quarterly Review* 384, 386, Professor Glanville Williams refers to " the vast and futile controversy concerning the proper meaning of the word ' law.' " I doubt whether the controversy has been futile because it may help us to understand what are the essential elements in these rules which govern the relationships of mankind. The pursuit of an adequate definition has led to a classification and analysis of the different types of rules which is as essential in political as it is in legal philosophy.

Force Theories of Law

It is convenient to begin with the *force* [11] theory of law because this is the one which has probably been the most widely accepted one in the past, and is still important today. It can be subdivided into the *command* theory and the *sanction* theory. These two theories are quite distinct although they both are based on physical force as an essential element in all law.

In England the command theory finds its source in Thomas Hobbes,[12] that frightened man who longed for a strong government in the tempestuous days of the seventeenth century, but it was given classic expression by John Austin in his famous *Lectures on Jurisprudence*.[13] He defined law as [14] " a rule laid down for the guidance of an intelligent being by an intelligent being having power over him." The key to the science of jurisprudence, he said, is the word *command*, because every law is a species of command. This command consists of the expression of a wish together with a sanction or evil which is attached to it in order to secure obedience. There can be no law therefore unless there is a specific person or group of persons who can express a wish, and who are prepared to enforce a sanction if the wish is disregarded.

---

[11] In his great work *Der Zweck im Recht*, von Ihering said that " law is the policy of force," and that " law is the aggregate of the coercive norms operative in a State."

[12] Hobbes defined law in *Leviathan*, Chap. 26, as : " And first it is manifest, that Law in generall, is not Counsell, but Command; nor a Command of any man to any man; but only of him, whose Command is addressed to one formerly obliged to obey him."

[13] These lectures were first published in 1861 after Austin's death.

[14] Lecture 1.

You will realise that this command definition of law is not a very attractive one. It assumes that in every law we must find a superior and an inferior, and it also assumes that the will of the superior is enforced on the inferior by the threat of a sanction. It is true that this law, like medicine, may be for the good of the individual who is bound by it, but at best it is a necessary evil. In Lecture IV Austin said,

" But the notion or idea of evil or imperfection is involved in the connected notions of law, duty and sanction. For, seeing that every law imposes a restraint, every law is an evil of itself: and, unless it be the work of malignity, or proceed from consummate folly, it also supposes an evil which it is designed to prevent or remedy. Law, like medicine, is a preventative or remedy of evil: and, if the world were free from evil, the notion and the name would be unknown."

It follows that as law is an evil of itself, it is only natural that anyone who is strong enough should attempt to avoid its effect. Force is therefore necessary to compel obedience, and, in the Austinian view, this may be said to be the foundation and inevitable basis of all law. If a sovereign cannot enforce his commands he ceases to be sovereign, and his commands lose the character of law, but as long as he has the power to govern, then his commands, unlimited and uncontrolled, are law. As Hobbes has said [15]: " Clubs are trumps."

[15] " In matter of government when nothing else is turned up, clubs are trumps ": 6 *Works* (ed. Molesworth, 1841) 122.

Austin and his most distinguished disciple Sir
Thomas Holland [16] did not deny that moral considerations might in certain instances influence the superior
in determining the content of the law, and that moral
considerations might help to persuade the inferior to
obey it, but this, they held, was irrelevant in any
interpretation of law itself: the stark fact remained
that law was nothing more than an expression of
physical force determining uniformity of conduct. The
great advantage of this definition, it was said, was
that it drew such a clear and absolute line between
law and morals. Thus Sir William Markby [17] argued
that the great virtue of this definition was that
" Austin by establishing the distinction between law
and morals . . . laid the foundation for a science of
law."

The attraction of the command theory lies in the
fact that it is a not inaccurate description of the typical
English statute. A statute appears to be a command
by a superior, the Queen-in-Parliament, to inferiors,
the Queen's subjects, which will be enforced by a
sanction if they fail to obey it. Even this is true only
of penal law where there may be said to be a direct
command to the subject. It is difficult to find a
command and a sanction in ordinary civil law. Thus
there is no command addressed to a testator requiring
him to make a will in a particular form because he is
free to make a will or not as he chooses. Nor can he
be threatened with a sanction because he will be dead
before the will can come into effect. If there is any

[16] *Elements of Jurisprudence*, 1880, 13th ed. (1924).
[17] *Elements of Law*, 6th ed. (1905), § 12.

command here then it is one addressed to the judge
directing him not to give legal effect to a will which
has not been properly executed. In this sense, and
only in this sense, all State law may be regarded as a
command addressed to the judges. But the moment
we go beyond the ordinary civil law we can see the
total inadequacy of this interpretation of law. It
leaves out the most important part of State law, *i.e.*,
constitutional law. It is obvious that the corner-stone
of the English legal system is the obedience that is
paid to the Queen-in-Parliament, but this cannot have
been commanded by anyone. The structure and the
authority of Parliament are based on a collection of
ancient and modern rules which, taken together, constitute the constitution, but they are based on
recognition and not on a non-existent command.

In a simple unitary State such as Great Britain it is
possible to ignore the importance of constitutional law
because there is rarely a dispute concerning any of its
provisions, and when such a dispute does arise it tends
to be regarded as a political rather than a legal
problem. But when we turn to the more complicated
systems of government which exist in federal States
such as the United States, Australia or Canada the
command definition becomes an impossible one. The
American constitution, which is the most important
single legal document in the history of the world,
clearly was not commanded by the Federal Convention
which drafted it, nor by the constituent States, nor by
the people of the United States. It was accepted as
a valid instrument of government, and it continues to
exist not by force, but by general recognition.

An interpretation of law which leaves out constitutional law seems to me to be clearly inadequate. But
that is not the only body of rules excluded by the
command theory. It also excludes all religious law,
except that which each of us believes to be the true
one, because those who think that there is a particular
Divinity may be in error. It is their belief that there
is a Divinity, and not His existence, which gives these
rules their compulsive character. Similarly international law, customary law, and moral law all fall
outside the scope of this interpretation because no one
has commanded them. A definition which ignores
history,[18] etymology,[19] and ordinary common sense
does not seem to be a particularly useful one.

In recent years this command interpretation of law
has been rejected by most jurists, largely on the
ground that a specific commander can be found in
hardly any legal systems, but it still has some
adherents.[20] In its place there has arisen the new

[18] The historical school of law, represented among others by Sir
Henry Maine in *Ancient Law* and by Pollock and Maitland in
History of English Law, has always repudiated the command
interpretation of law as it is clearly not applicable to early
law. The anthropologists, *e.g.*, Malinowski in *Crime and
Custom in Savage Society*, have also repudiated it. We shall
see that this criticism is also applicable to the sanction theory.

[19] Professor E. C. Clark in his little-known, but valuable, book
Practical Jurisprudence (1883) pointed out (p. 90) that " the
unconscious definitions of law furnished by those early names
for it ' were a useful guide.' That which is *fitting, orderly*
or *regular* (*jus*); that which is *observed* (*witoth*); that which is
from everlasting (*oew*)—these are the earliest ideas of law
which we can find in the language of the Romans, the Goths,
and the Anglo-Saxons or early English.'' Not one of them
includes any element of command or sanction.

[20] R. A. Eastwood and G. W. Keeton, *Austinian Theories of
Law and Sovereignty* (1929). This is the most convincing
modern interpretation of the Austinian doctrine.

" Pure Theory of Law " which Professor Kelsen has made famous throughout the world.[21]   In place of the word *command* as the key to the science of jurisprudence this school substitutes the word *sanction*. We still find that force is the dominant element in law although it has assumed a new, and much more complicated, guise.   Every positive legal order is based on a basic norm which " is nothing but the fundamental rule according to which the various norms of the order are to be created." [22]   This basic norm " is presupposed to be valid because without this presupposition no human act could be interpreted as a legal, especially as a norm-creating act." [23]   The subsidiary norms must all be " measures of coercion " [24] which provide for sanctions because " by this very fact and only by this fact, that is, by this specific social technique is it distinguished from other social orders." [25]   The distinction between law, which is a coercive order, and voluntary obedience is " that one provides measures of coercion as sanctions whereas the other does not." [26]   The subsidiary norm does not, however, depend for its validity on the efficacy of its sanction: " A norm is not valid *because* it is efficacious; it is valid *if* the order to which it belongs is, on the whole, efficacious." [27]

[21] I shall refer in particular to his *General Theory of Law and State*, 1949.
[22] p. 114.
[23] p. 116.
[24] p. 18.
[25] p. 25.
[26] p. 19.
[27] p. 42.

Like the *command* theory of law the *sanction* theory of law finds its attraction in the fact that it is a more or less accurate description of ordinary civil law, *i.e.*, the statutes enacted by the legislature and the precedent-rules established by the courts are subsidiary norms under the basic norm. In most of them we can find a sanction although sometimes this requires considerable logical ingenuity. But when we turn to constitutional law, to customary or primitive law, to international law, or to religious law the *sanction* theory is as inadequate as the *command* theory. It does not attempt to explain the existence of the basic norm on which the whole legal system is founded: this we must presuppose because otherwise " no human act would be interpreted as legal." But without an adequate foundation no legal system can stand, just as a house without a foundation will collapse, so that a theory of law which merely takes this foundation for granted can be of little value.

The lack of reality in Kelsen's theory seems to me to be illustrated by his statement that a legal order to be valid must on the whole be efficacious, but that the particular norms need have no efficacy provided they contain a formal sanction. What Kelsen fails to explain is how a legal order can be efficacious unless its subsidiary norms are obeyed, because a legal order can act only through subsidiary norms. It is difficult therefore to understand why Kelsen places so much emphasis on the sanction. As the norm need not be efficacious it follows that the sanction need only be a formal one. The sanction seems to be used to distinguish law from other types of rules, which are baser imitations, just as a hall-mark is used to distinguish silver from other metals. No one would, however, regard the statement that a silver teapot can be distinguished from a plate one because the former bears a hall-mark as an adequate definition of silver, although it may be useful from the purely practical point of view. The important point to note is that if the sanction need only be formal then it cannot be an essential element in law.

The most serious objection to the Pure Theory of Law is that it keeps us from seeing the essential difference between a coercive order and an obligatory order. We are led to regard the two words as synonymous. When Kelsen says that a *coercive order* must provide a measure of coercion he is making a self-evident statement, but it does not follow from this that an *obligatory order* must provide a measure of coercion because it may be regarded as obligatory without coercion. In ordinary life we realise that there may be all the difference in the world between coercion and obligation : it is essential to remember that the same difference is of importance in our inter-pretation of law. It is because a rule is regarded as obligatory that a measure of coercion may be attached to it : it is not obligatory because there is coercion. A theory of law which makes coercion an essential element in its interpretation seems to me therefore to be misleading. It is true that Kelsen seeks to meet this objection by saying that he is speaking of a normative order under which the person commanding is " authorised " or " empowered " to issue commands

of a binding nature.[28]   This authorisation comes from
the basic norm which cannot itself be coercive, *viz.*,
based on a sanction.   By blandly suggesting that this
basic norm must be " presupposed to be binding "
Kelsen avoids the most important problem in legal
philosophy.   It reminds one of the dreamer who goes
into great detail about what he is going to do with a
million pounds, but when asked where he is going to
get his million pounds says that that is a practical
question with which he is not concerned.

OBLIGATION THEORY OF LAW

Having rejected both the command and the sanction
theories of law I must now attempt to give my own
interpretation.   Although I shall frame it in my own
words I cannot claim that it is original because it is
borrowed in large part from Sir Frederick Pollock,[29]
whose contributions to the philosophy of law have
never been sufficiently appreciated, perhaps because
they were made in so lucid a manner.   After pointing
out that [30] history shows that law precedes the
organised society which we know as a State and that
it can exist without a formal sanction, he concludes

[28] At p. 31 Kelsen says: " To repeat: A command is binding,
not because the individual commanding has an actual
superiority in power, but because he is ' authorised ' or ' empowered ' to issue commands of a binding nature.   And he is
' authorised ' or ' empowered ' only if a normative order, which
is presupposed to be binding, confers on him this capacity, the
competence to issue binding commands."
[29] Pollock's *A First Book of Jurisprudence*, 1896, 5th ed., 1923, is
his only book directly concerned with legal philosophy.   His
various essays are, however, of equal importance, especially his
often-quoted one on the " History of the Law of Nature."
[30] p. 24.

that [31]: "Law is enforced by the State because it is law; it is not law merely because the State enforces it." A rule of law is " a rule conceived as binding."[32]

Austin found the key to the science of jurisprudence in the word *command*: I suggest that a more correct view is to find it in the word *obligation*. I should therefore define law as any rule of human conduct which is recognised as being obligatory. It is distinguished from a purely voluntary rule of human conduct which is followed for its own sake: thus if a man always puts on an overcoat in winter to avoid the cold he is not following this course of conduct because of any sense of obligation. Under the word *rule* I include, for the sake of brevity, those principles or standards which are regarded as binding even though they may not be as exact as a prescribed regulation. Although these principles are flexible in their application, nevertheless they are sufficiently determinate to be regarded as part of the legal system.

It is essential to draw a clear distinction between obedience to an order or a rule and recognition that the order or rule is obligatory, *i.e.*, that the order or rule *ought* to be obeyed. We may obey an order solely because we fear that if we do not do so we shall incur an evil. In such a case we are reacting to naked force, and we shall seek to avoid obedience if that is possible. We have no conative feeling: no sense that we are under a duty of any nature. On the other hand, if we recognise that a rule is obligatory our reaction will be entirely different. It is true that we

[31] p. 29.
[32] p. 26.

may refuse to perform our obligation either because we feel that there is some other conflicting obligation of greater strength or for some selfish reason, but nevertheless the feeling of *oughtness* will remain. There is a vast difference between obedience to force and obedience to law, and if we fail to understand this then we shall misinterpret the history of England, and we shall ignore the greatest contribution which this country has made to the civilisation of the world. Let me give you one illustration to make my point. A gangster enters a bank, and orders, at the point of his gun, all the persons there to raise their hands. A police constable, who is present, calls on them, as he is entitled to do under the common law, to assist him in arresting the gangster. Why do we regard the gangster's order as an arbitrary command and the police constable's order as a legal one? The answer obviously does not depend on any sanction, because the sanction behind the gangster's order is far more powerful than is any which the law can apply. Even if we obey the gangster because of fear, we know that in doing so we are violating our obligation to the Crown,—we have broken the law. I believe that in no other country in the world is this obligation recognised more clearly than in England, and that the strength of the law is in large part based on this. It is this which brings even a nursemaid to the support of the police, as happened when the murderers of Field-Marshal Sir Henry Wilson tried to escape in 1922. The recognition of this obligation may be an unconscious one but this is merely evidence of how deeply ingrained it is. People may carry out a command because they are afraid not to do so, but it does not become a law for them unless they recognise that there is an obligation on them to obey. If this were not so then it would never be possible to distinguish between law and arbitrary command.

If, then, it is not fear of evil which makes a rule obligatory, what grounds can we find for this sense of obligation? This question has been discussed by few legal philosophers because it is sufficient for their purposes that the sense of obligation exists.[33] Thus Sir Frederick Pollock, after stating that law is a rule conceived as binding, says that,[34] " the further pursuit of this subject seems to belong to the philosophy of Politics rather than of Law." I cannot, however,

[33] Lord Bryce in his essay on " Obedience " in his *Studies in History and Jurisprudence*, 1901, Vol. II, 463, sums up the motives of compliance under five heads in the order of their importance—indolence, deference, sympathy, fear, reason. It is important to note that what Bryce is discussing is *obedience* and not *obligation*. Thus indolence may be a motive for obedience, but it cannot be a ground on which the recognition of obligation can be based.

Similary Rudolf Stammler is speaking about obedience and not about obligation when he says in *The Theory of Justice*:
" Law presents itself as an external regulation of human conduct. By this we understand the laying down of norms which are quite independent of the person's inclination to follow them. It is immaterial whether a person obeys them because he regards them as right, submitting out of respect for the law; or whether his obedience is due to a selfish motive of some sort, fear of punishment, or hope of reward; or, finally, whether he thinks about it at all, or acts from mere habit."
It is remarkable to find a legal philosopher accepting the view that it is immaterial whether a person submits out of respect for the law or out of fear. All those who live under the common law may reflect with some pride that Anglo-American history is in large part meaningless unless the distinction between the two is realised.

[34] p. 29.

avoid this difficult question because in these lectures I am concerned with the effect that moral law may exert in producing the feeling of *oughtness* which I regard as an essential element in our concept of law.

It is necessary to say only a few words concerning the nature of the obligation recognised by the person who may establish the law—the commander, who under the Austinian definition is all-important. From his standpoint it is unnecessary to go beyond the fact that he recognises his own authority—whether rightful or wrongful in origin is immaterial—to lay down the law. By establishing the law he recognises that others are under an obligation to obey. The fact that he has declared it is sufficient to make it obligatory in his own eyes. As a general rule he may attach a threatened sanction to the law in case it should not be obeyed, but this cannot be necessary to give it validity so far as he himself is concerned. A dying, powerless king may still issue a law. An exiled government, which may realise that no effective sanction can be attached to its orders, may nevertheless hold that they are valid and binding, and that they ought to be obeyed by those to whom they are addressed.[35]

The view of the person establishing the law is, however, of only slight juridical interest because, as I have said, there may be no person establishing the

---

[35] In my article " An Apology for Jurisprudence " in *Interpretations of Modern Legal Philosophies*, ed. Paul Sayre, Oxford University Press, 1947, I discussed this question at greater length, with special reference to the decrees issued by the Royal Netherlands Government in London during the recent war.

law, as, for example, in the case of constitutional law. But even if there is such a person, or group of persons, as in the case of the ordinary statute, it is the recognition by others which is important. It does not matter what the Members of Parliament think concerning their own authority. They themselves can do nothing. What makes the statute effective—what turns it from a mere collection of words into a law— is the recognition of its validity by others. This recognition is of a double character. The first recognition is by the officers of the State—the judges, the sheriffs, and the police—who enforce the statute. The second recognition is by the ordinary members of the State who obey the law. Why, for example, do 40,000,000 people recognise that they are under an obligation to obey a statute enacted by a comparatively few elderly gentlemen sitting in the Palace of Westminster? A similar question arises whenever we are considering the foundation on which any other body of law, such as religious law or customary law, is based.

The most important ground on which this recognition of obligation is based is also the least precise. In a book of great interest, recently translated by Professor Broad of Cambridge University, the Swedish Professor Axel Hägerström [36] emphasised that it is " the general law conviction " within a particular society which gives a rule of conduct its obligatory

---

[36] *Inquiries Into the Nature of Law and Morals.* 1953. Edited by Karl Olivecrona. Translated by C. D. Broad. 1953. Almquist and Wiksell, Stockholm.

nature.[37] This "law conviction" may be based on various grounds which may not be understood by the people who are governed by it. A felt conviction may, however, be more powerful than one which is rationalised. Perhaps the strongest influence may be the vague feeling of duty arising from the habits of the people. It is because a rule has been long established that the majority of persons in a society may recognise it as obligatory. The jurist cannot ignore this "law conviction" because if he does so then his theories will lack reality.

A second ground on which the feeling of obligation is based is that of reverence. This is, of course, strongest in the case of religious law because here the duty of obedience is based on reverence for God. This feeling may be of similar importance in other legal systems. In his famous book *The English Constitution* Walter Bagehot, writing during the reign of Queen Victoria, pointed out how great a role the Monarchy plays in the British system of government. He said [38]:

> "The English Monarchy strengthens our govern-
> ment with the strength of religion. It is not easy
> to say why it should be so. Every instructed

[37] He said at p. 65: "Suppose we take the phrase ' general law conviction in a society ' to mean a conviction that so-and-so is a law which is binding on the society as a whole. And suppose we take this latter expression to mean that it is a rule which lays down rights and duties and also the way in which they are to be enforced if they should be infringed. Then the ' general conviction of law in a society ' makes such a rule into a positive law, in the sense of a rule which is actually applied—in the last resort through coercion on the part of the legal organs."

[38] Chap. 2, The Monarchy.

theologian would say that it was the duty of a
person born under a Republic as much to obey
that Republic as it is the duty of one born under a
Monarchy to obey the monarch. But the mass of
the English people do not think so; they agree with
the oath of allegiance; they say it is their duty to
obey the " Queen," and they have but hazy notions
as to obeying laws without a queen."

This is an illustration of the powerful part which
reverence can play in establishing the sense of legal
obligation.

A third ground is the recognition that law is
essential if we are to escape from anarchy. Consciously or unconsciously the people realise that
without fixed rules civilised life will come to an end.
It is this feeling which is of such advantage to those
who seize power by force. It explains the rapidity
with which a usurper becomes a recognised ruler.
Even in war-time the invader is recognised as having
authority to maintain and establish rules for the
ordinary conduct of civilian life. That this recognition is not based on force or fear is shown by the fact
that even after the invader has been driven out the
validity of acts done under these rules will be
recognised.

Finally there is the recognition that there is a moral
obligation to obey the rule. This recognition may
take two different forms. The first is the moral
obligation to obey the rules as such. Thus there is a
moral obligation to obey any law issued by the
Government merely because it has been issued. This

moral obligation is not an absolute one for in certain circumstances other conflicting moral obligations may be felt to have greater force. It is based on the realisation that without law the State will collapse, and that all its members will suffer. It is a moral duty which is not owed to the State as such but to one's fellow-men. The second form of moral obligation arises when it is recognised that the rule is intrinsically right and just. It is self-evident that this must greatly influence the sense of obligation which a man feels in regard to a rule which binds him, but it is less frequently noted how strong is this feeling where others are concerned. We may recognise that a rule is obligatory because it is right that other persons should be bound. My recognition of the obligatory nature of the law of contract may be based as much on my recognition that there is a duty on the other man to fulfil his promise to me as it is on the recognition of a similar duty binding on me.[39] This feeling that it is right that others should be bound is more than a selfish one: without it the force of law may lose its strength. In his famous book, *Der Kampf ums Recht,* von Ihering went so far as to say that it was the duty of the holder of a legal right to seek its enforcement against anyone who had violated it, because surrender to such a violation weakened the whole conception of law. Unfortunately von Ihering did not emphasise sufficiently that it is even more important to seek the enforcement of one's neighbour's rights. The strength of law in a nation depends to a large extent on the determination shown

[39] *Cf.* Edmond N. Cahn, *The Sense of Injustice,* 1949.

by its members that the rights of even the least deserving should be preserved.

There are undoubtedly other grounds on which the recognition of legal obligation may be founded but I believe that the ones I have discussed are the principal ones. You will have noticed that I have left out fear which the force theory of law places in the forefront. This has not been due to an oversight on my part. Fear, as I have said, may produce obedience to a command, as in the case of a bandit, but it cannot bring about a sense of obligation. If we do not understand this distinction then we cannot differentiate between rule by force and rule by law.

It may be argued that my conception of law leads to the absurd result that a man who does not recognise that he is bound by the law against murder ought not to be regarded as subject to it. The answer to this is that when we talk of the law of a country we are not concerned with the views of particular individuals. We are concerned with the general sense of obligation held by those who are enforcing what they recognise to be the law. Thus when we are asked " What is English law on a particular subject ? " we can answer this by stating what the judges recognise to be the law, but when we are asked the further question " Why have the judges got this authority ? " we can answer only by saying that this is recognised to be part of the British Constitution by the people of England. Thus Dicey's definition of law in his *Conflict of Laws* [40] as the rules recognised by the courts

[40] First published in 1896. 4th ed., p. 5.

is useful as a practical test, but it is scientifically inadequate as it does not refer to the basic question concerning the authority of the judges. Why, for example, does the Anglo-American law give its judges greater power in this regard than does the Continental law to its judges?

If the force or sanction interpretation of law is the correct one then it is clear that the influence of moral ideas on the law can be regarded as of minor importance. The essential element then is an exercise of force in the application of the sanction. If, on the other hand, we regard law as a rule which is recognised as obligatory then the element of force becomes of minor importance. We then realise that the obligatory nature of these rules is based on other grounds, and that one of the most important of these is that of moral law. It is for this reason that the moral sense is one of the dominant forces not only in establishing the efficacy of law, but also in its very existence. The jurist cannot ignore the moral law as irrelevant to his subject because if he does so then he will be ignoring one of the grounds on which the basic idea of obligation is based. It is therefore necessary for me to turn now to a consideration of the moral law, and to the various meanings which have been ascribed to that phrase.

MORAL LAW

The Oxford Dictionary defines *moral* as " concerned with character or disposition, or with the distinction between right and wrong." In the first sense we are talking about the moral character of the individual.

He may be said to be moral if he acts in accordance
with what he believes to be right, and to be immoral
if his purpose or motive is wrongful.[41] It is obvious
that used in this sense there can be no objective moral
law because each person must be a law unto himself
in deciding what he believes is right or wrong.
According to this interpretation of morality the obligation is to do what the conscience of the individual
person tells him is right. It has therefore been said [42]
that " morality works from within outwards and it is
this *internal* character which distinguishes it from the
law of the land and the conventions of society." This
subjective interpretation compels the jurist to disregard morality almost completely, for if morality
depends on the conscience of each individual then no
general rules, whether legal or otherwise, can be based
on it.

There is another school of thought, however, which
rejects this subjective interpretation of the moral law,
and accepts an objective one. " The suggestion,"
Mr. Kneale has said in a valuable essay,[43] " that
sentences about obligation, rightness and wrongness
have no objective reference sticks in our throats . . .
the important question is whether such judgments can
be true or false in the ordinary sense." He reaches
the conclusion that moral judgments " are not merely
expressions of our own preferences or those of our

---

[41] Thus Rudolph Stammler in *The Theory of Justice*, p. 141,
    says: " Law presents itself as an external regulation of
    human conduct. . . . Ethical theory is concerned with the
    question of the content of a man's own will, in whose heart
    there must be no opposition of being and seeming."
[42] Winfield, *Select Legal Essays*, 1953, p. 267.
[43] *Objectivity in Morals* (1950) Philosophy, 149, 151.

group, but applications of a law to which all men commit themselves when they claim to be reasonable." [44]   Reason alone cannot, however, determine the content of the moral law because " reason is not a motive for anything, and so not a motive for the making of the moral law." [45]   We must therefore, he says, introduce a notion of sympathy to explain the motive of moral law.

If we accept, as I do, Mr. Kneale's conclusion that it is correct to speak of an objective moral law then we must ask the question—where do we find this objective moral law ? The answer to this question is of the utmost interest at the present time because, as I hope to show in the remaining lectures, our moral conclusions are of basic importance in the formation of our law. In a static period when both law and morals are accepted as more or less fixed it will not be so necessary to analyse our moral concepts, but when our State law is changing it is then necessary for us to seek for a true interpretation of the moral law with which it is so closely associated. I believe that the so-called revival of " natural law " thinking at the present time is merely an expression of this point of view. It is because we recognise that law cannot be explained in terms of force that we seek to find the moral law which tends to give it its strength.

As the classic phrase " law of nature " is so highly charged with emotion and has meant so many different things at various times in history, I think that it is preferable to speak of moral law instead.

[44] p. 163.
[45] p. 161.

This does not, however, take us very far because there are different views concerning the basis of this moral law. Here again I believe that it is the idea of obligation which is the essential element. In moral law, as in other types of law, the primary question is why do people regard the moral law as obligatory?

The first concept of moral law is as an expression of the will of God. It can be found either in the explicit commands of the Divine Being, as for example in certain of the Ten Commandments, or in the implied commands which can be discovered through reason. By the application of reason to the basic premises of the religion we can obtain an answer to every moral question. As a religion must from its very nature accept its basic tenets as permanent and unalterable, it follows that a moral law based on these truths will tend to be equally permanent and unalterable. The view that there is an absolute objective moral law which applies at all times and under all circumstances is a resultant of this doctrine.[46] Thus if a religion provides that a man shall have no more than one wife it follows that this rule will be regarded by the members of that religion as a moral law, obligatory on all men, whether they are members of that religious body or not. The moral law recognised by the believers in one religion may therefore differ in a radical manner from that recognised by the believers

[46] W. D. Lamont, *Principles of Moral Judgment*, 1946, p. 4: "If a person holds that the final standard of right and wrong is the Divine will as interpreted by the church, then the 'moral' and the 'religious' judgments will for him be identical."

in another.[47]   Mr. Kneale has said that " the notion
of a specific moral law seems to be inseparably bound
up with the policy of mutual tolerance," [48] but this is
exceedingly doubtful when the moral law has its
foundation in religion because this religious moral law
must on certain points be absolute.   The strength of
the belief in the obligatory nature of this religious
moral law will necessarily depend on the strength of
the belief in the religion itself.   Of all the grounds on
which the obligatory nature of the moral law has been
based this is the most potent one, because it is based
on the authority of a Divine Being.   Being both
absolute and strong it is the one which is likely to
have the most persuasive influence on State law, and
is also the one which may come into most direct
conflict with it.

---

[47] Two recent books are of great interest from this standpoint.
In *Law and the Laws*, 1952, Dr. Nathaniel Micklem states
what may be described as a Protestant Christian law of
nature.   He takes the view (p. 59) that " law is neither ethics
nor religion but law is not safe, it is not even law, when it is
divorced from ethics and religion."   Again he says (at p. 114):
" We cannot reject the religion of the Bible and permanently
retain our law and justice."   In referring to international law,
he says (p. 95): " International law as we understand it rests
broadly upon the Christian ethic and is only conceivable on
that basis."   On the other hand, he disagrees with the Roman
Catholic law of nature as stated in Fr. Watt's *The Natural
Rights of Man*, especially (p. 83) concerning private property.
Concerning freedom of conscience he says (p. 88): " Fr. Watt
is probably concerned with the claim of a ' natural right ' to
be a good Roman Catholic; his Church does not believe that
anyone has a ' natural right ' to be a Protestant or unbeliever."
  The Roman Catholic doctrine concerning the law of nature
has been stated by Professor d'Entrèves in his brilliant book
Natural Law, 1951.   It contains a profound and lucid analysis
of the various schools of thought throughout the ages.   It also
gives a fair statement of the influence that this doctrine has
had.   [48] *Op. cit.*, n. 43, at p. 164.

The second ground on which the moral law has been based is intuition or instinct.[49] In this interpretation natural moral law is closely akin to natural physical law. It is an expression of uniform human feelings, and it holds that because these feelings exist they must be right. Thus, to take the most obvious example, the fact that most parents are prepared to care for their children is held to be proof that it is a moral duty that parents must care for their children. Again, the institution of private property is given a natural moral law foundation, on the ground that even primitive man will fight to retain a thing which he has seized. Similarly, it is said that even a young child will lay a special claim to a thing which he has been the first to possess. In his bitter attack on the idea of a law of nature Bentham[50] pointed out that because men are inclined to act in a particular way, it does not necessarily follow that it is morally right for them to act in that way. There is, of course, truth in this criticism, but the criticism is based on a misconception of the argument. If the natural instincts of human beings tended to be destructive of

[49] This has been stated in its most famous form by Ulpian, *Digest*, 1.1.3, repeated in the *Institutes*, I, 2.: "Natural law is that which all animals have been taught by nature; this law is not peculiar to the human species, it is common to all animals which are produced on land or sea, and to birds of the air as well. From it comes the union of man and woman called matrimony, and therewith the procreation of children; we find in fact that animals in general, the very wild beasts, are marked by acquaintance with this law."

[50] In *The Theory of Legislation*, p. 167, Bentham said: "Parents are inclined to support their children; parents ought to support their children; these are two distinct propositions. The first does not suppose the second; the second does not suppose the first."

the human race then it would have ceased to exist long
ago.   There is, therefore, at least a presumption that
the human instincts, if not carried to excess, tend
to the preservation of the race and to the good of
mankind.   It is therefore not absurd to suggest that
our instinctive feeling is some guide to objective moral
law.   Here again this concept of moral law tends to
influence State law because the latter will gain
strength if it is in accord with what people
instinctively feel is right.

The third school bases moral law on reason.   When
we speak of reason in this connection we mean logical
deductions from a basic premise.   We must therefore
find the basic premise on which this moral law of
reason can be founded.   If our basic premise is
grounded on the view that all men are wicked and are
not to be trusted, then we shall get a peculiarly
warped moral law.   I think that this explains the
extraordinary conclusions reached by Machiavelli and
Hobbes.   Thus, in the eighteenth chapter of *The
Prince*, Nicolo Machiavelli discusses " The Way
Princes Should Keep Faith," and he reaches the
conclusion that they should not do so if it is against
their interest.   " If men were entirely good this pre-
cept would not hold, but because they are bad, and
will not keep faith with you, you too are not bound
to observe it with them."   If it is true that men are
bad then his conclusion that there is no duty to keep
faith with them is perfectly reasonable.   The result is
that morality disappears and only force remains.
Thomas Hobbes took an equally gloomy view of
natural man.   Unless law is established by force men,

he held, can have no conception of right or wrong. In *Leviathan* he said [51]:

> " Hereby it is manifest, that during the time men live without a common Power to keep them all in awe, they are in that condition which is called Warre; and such a warre, as is of every man, against every man. . . . To this warre of every man against every man, this also is consequent; that nothing can be Unjust. The notions of Right and Wrong, Justice and Injustice have there no place. Where there is no common Power, there is no Law: where no Law, no Injustice. Force, and Fraud, are in warre the two Cardinall vertues."

Here again, if men are by nature of such a brutish character, the only instrument which will be able to control them is brute force.

On the other hand, if we accept as our basic premise that, as man is a social animal, it is natural and right for him to seek to benefit his fellow-men, it then becomes the basic premise of this moral law that a man shall love and not hate his neighbour. It is true that this basic premise is only a value judgment and that it is impossible to prove by reason that the opposite conclusion is not equally correct. But having accepted this value judgment, it is then possible to develop by reason certain moral rules. The rational man must realise that there are rules of conduct which are necessary for the good life both of the individual and of the community. Reason teaches us that we must not kill, or steal, or lie if we wish to benefit our fellow-men, because each of these acts will

[51] Part I, Chap. 13.

tend to their injury. This was expressed by Cicero in *De Legibus* [52] in these words: " For where then will there be a place for generosity, or love of country, or loyalty, or the inclination to be of service to others or to show gratitude for favours received? For these virtues originate in our natural inclination to love our fellow-men, and this is the foundation of justice." Hugo Grotius seeks this same foundation for International Law in his *De Jure Belli et Pacis* [53]: " And among these properties which are peculiar to man, is a desire for society; that is a desire for a life spent in common with fellow-men; and not merely spent somehow, but spent tranquilly, and in a manner corresponding to the character of his intellect. . . And therefore the assertion, that, by nature, every animal is impelled only to seek its own advantage or good, if stated so generally as to include man, cannot be conceded." This moral law, based on reason, is a relative rather than an absolute one, because what may be reasonable under one set of circumstances may not be reasonable under another. The theory of a natural law with a changing content, which has been especially popular with legal philosophers, is an example of this doctrine. It may be said that this interpretation of moral law is closely akin to the utilitarian doctrine. It cannot be denied that in certain regards it is utilitarian, but it is a utilitarianism based on sympathy for others rather than on regard for oneself. I am not, however, concerned with the question whether this view of the moral law can be theoretically justified. The important point is

[52] I, 15, 43.   [53] Vol. I, Prolegomena, p. xlii, s. 6,

that it has been accepted by a great number of men, and that it has played a leading part in the development of law.

In practice we are unlikely to find that any clear line is drawn between the three kinds of " natural law." They have the same aim because each of them seeks to provide an ideal test for the existing law. It may be said that in family law cases including marriage, divorce and responsibility for children, one finds more frequent references to the religious natural law than in other branches.[54] The type of moral law based on reason, divorced from other authority, seems to be the one which has had most influence in English law. It is to the reason of the case that the judges, even in Equity, have given most weight. It is a pragmatic natural law and not one based on general principles expressed in authoritative sources.

I may perhaps summarise this lecture by saying that I have attempted to show that law is a rule of conduct which is recognised as being obligatory. This sense of obligation is based on various grounds, including that of morality. In English law we shall, I think, find that morality has played a particularly important part in the development of the common law, and that on the whole we shall be able to say at the conclusion of these lectures that English law and the moral law are rarely in conflict.

[54] As these lectures are limited to the influence which the moral law has had on English law it has not been within their scope to discuss the influence of religious law as such. The judgments of the House of Lords in *Bowman* v. *Secular Society* [1917] A.C. 406, in which their Lordships had to determine the question whether the common law incorporated the rules of the Christian religion, are therefore not directly in point here.

CONSTITUTIONAL LAW,
ADMINISTRATIVE LAW
AND
INTERNATIONAL LAW

2

CONSTITUTIONAL LAW, ADMINISTRATIVE LAW AND INTERNATIONAL LAW

In my first lecture I have defined law in general as a rule of conduct which is recognised as being obligatory. It is obvious that this definition must cover a very wide field. Most of us recognise that we are under an obligation to obey the rules of our religion, of our State, of the various societies to which we belong such as a university or a social club, and the rules which we recognise as constituting the moral law. Is there any test by which we can draw a distinction between these various types of law? In particular, what is the element which enables us to draw a clear line of demarcation between religious law, moral law, and State or civil law,[1] for these are of peculiar importance in controlling the lives of all men?

It has been suggested by Professor Kelsen that the distinction between these various rules lies in the nature of the sanction. State law, according to his view, is an order which is distinguished by its specific technique in that it provides a sanction directed against the member of the community who does not fulfil his duty. " The law does this by providing that if a man commits murder, then another man, designated by the legal order, shall apply against the

---

[1] The term " civil law " is usually used as a synonym for State law. It may also be used to describe modern Roman law, or that part of State law which is not penal.

murderer a certain measure of coercion, prescribed by the legal order." [2] On the other hand, morality, it is said, limits itself to requiring: Thou shalt not kill. Thus, the moral reaction against immoral conduct is neither provided by the moral order, nor, if provided, is it socially organised. Religious norms resemble legal norms in that they provide a sanction, but this is of a transcendental character and not socially organised. With all respect to Professor Kelsen, I believe that this distinction based on the nature of the sanction is an invalid one. In early law the same tribunal may be purporting to administer religious law, moral law and State law. [3] There is no reason why religious law should not be enforced by an earthly tribunal, even though the ultimate punishment may be a transcendental one. Similarly, the breach of moral law may entail the sanction of expulsion from the community, even though there is no formal machinery by which this sanction can be enforced. The sanction which in fact makes certain State laws effective may not be the sanction which the law itself provides. Thus, during the recent war, the effectiveness of many of the rules prohibiting the purchase of food and of goods on the black market was due, not to the fines provided by the rules themselves, but to the social stigma which was attached to the breach of these rules. Having been concerned in a small way

[2] p. 20.
[3] *Cf.* Pound, *Law and Morals*, p. 29: "We begin, then with a condition of undifferentiated social control—as we should have said in the last century, a condition of undifferentiated religion, morals and law—in which law, as we now think of it, that is, social control through the force of politically organised society, is the least in scope and the least in efficacy of the three."

with the administration of these rules,[4] I am convinced that they would have been very nearly as effective as they were if no sanction had been attached to them, because all that was required was the creation of a tribunal which could establish that the rules had been violated. It was the fear of social disapproval, and not the inadequate fines which secured almost universal compliance.[5]

Unlike the sanction theory of law, the command theory of law bases its distinction on the source of the command. Religious law is the command of God, State law is the command of the sovereign, and moral law is not law at all because there is no commander.[6] This interpretation of law, as I suggested in the first lecture, is totally inadequate even when applied to State law, because we can never find any person or group of persons who commands the constitution. Moreover, it fails to recognise the fact that the same person may be purporting to enforce all three types of law in primitive administration. This may continue even when the degree of civilisation has reached a comparatively high standard. Thus Professor Pound has said [7]:

[4] I was chairman of the Southern Region Price Regulation Committee.
[5] In his stimulating book, *The Law In Quest Of Itself*, Professor Fuller repudiates the " bad man " interpretation of law suggested by Mr. Justice Holmes in one of his lighter moments. Fuller says (p. 93): " it is a peculiar sort of bad man who is worried about judicial decrees and is indifferent to extra-legal penalties, who is concerned about a fine of two dollars but apparently not about the possible loss of friends and customers." My experience fully supports this criticism.
[6] Austin, *Jurisprudence*, Chap. I.
[7] *Social Control Through Law*, p. 18.

" The major agencies of social control are morals, religion, and law. In the beginnings of law these are not differentiated. Even in so advanced a civilisation as that of the Greek city-state the same word is used to mean religious rites, ethical custom, the traditional course of adjusting relations, the legislation of the city, and all of these looked on as a whole; as we should say, including all these agencies of social control under the one term which we now translate law."

If then we cannot draw a distinction between the different types of law either because of the nature of the sanction, or because of the nature of the command, is there any other method by which we can draw such a line? I believe that there is a clear distinction based not on form but on substance. The distinction between them is based on the nature of the duty which is recognised to exist. The distinction can be stated as follows: —

1. Religious law consists of those rules which are recognised as stating the duty which is owed to the Divine Being. It does not matter from the juridical standpoint whether the religion is true or false. These rules are obligatory, and therefore law, for those who believe that they express a duty to God, but they are not law for those who do not so believe. The efficacy of religious law depends on the strength of the belief in the existence of the Supreme Being, and not on the strength of any sanction. It is a gloomy interpretation of human nature to suggest that these rules are regarded as obligatory merely because of a threat

of future punishment. This is fear and not devotion. The fact that the belief in Hell is no longer an essential part of religion ought not to weaken the sense of obligation to the Creator.

In religious law the primary duty is to God, although this law may also prescribe a duty to others. In such a case the breach of a duty to others also entails the breach of a duty to God. Similarly, religious law may prescribe a duty of obedience to those in authority in a State. An act of disobedience in these circumstances violates two duties, one religious and one civil, and two different types of law. Thus, those who believed in the Divine Right of Kings held that a double duty of obedience was owed to the King—one religious and one civil.

2. Moral law consists of those rules of conduct which are recognised as obligatory in regard to one's fellow-men. In so far as ethics is concerned with the subjective goodness or badness of an act and its effect on the conscience of the actor it lies outside the field of law. As I have already suggested, the obligation recognised in moral law may find its origin in various different and sometimes conflicting sources. When there is a conflict, the moral law becomes of doubtful validity. Religious law when it is concerned with man's duty to his fellow-men, reason which makes it clear that no society can exist unless each member owes a duty to the others, and the innate " love of one's neighbour " which makes man a social animal, all combine to found the recognition of a moral law. Perhaps strongest of all are the traditional habits or *mores* of the group which tend to be

regarded as obligatory merely because they have been established for a long period.[8] Age gives authority not only to men but also to their practices. The former must die and are buried, but the latter may continue to rule us for an unlimited time. Moral law, far from being uncertain and weak because it has no commander and no definite sanction, may be as precise and even more powerful than any rule which we call State law.

3. State law can be briefly defined as those rules of conduct which are recognised as being obligatory on the members of the society which we call by the name *State*. This definition is obviously incomplete until we have established the nature of this particular society and who are its members.

The State is a society of men, living within a particular territory, directed to a particular purpose. It differs from other societies because of its purpose and not by the form which it assumes or because of the machinery which it operates. I do not agree with Austin that a State must consist of a sovereign and subjects, nor do I agree with Kelsen that the machinery with which the State operates—a rule to which a sanction is attached—is peculiar to the State. Nor do I believe that the State is a political organisation "because it monopolises the use of

---

[8] Hägerström, p. 39, speaks of "the inherited custom of observing what is called the law of the land." He continues, "Such factors as custom and the feeling that it is natural to observe the existing legal rules have great influence; and they give rise to actions in the mass of the people, by which the law is maintained without any will intervening."

force." [9] If this statement is taken literally it is obviously untrue because there may be other organisations within a State which may have more physical force than the State can command. As long as these organisations recognise their obligation to the State and are prepared to support it this is all that is necessary. Nor does the theory of the State need such a monopoly: all that it requires is that the purpose of the State shall be the maintenance of order. This can be secured either by the exercise of force directly under the control of the State or by the exercise of extraneous force acting in support of the State. The trouble with phrases concerning the " monopoly of force " is that they suggest that the State must make itself physically all-powerful if it is to survive. States have assumed an infinite variety of forms, but nevertheless they have one essential element in common, and that element we find in the purpose of the society. This is not surprising because all other societies are defined by the function they are to perform and not by any other fact. Thus, a trade union is a society whose purpose it is to protect all its members in matters of wages and conditions of work, musical societies are organised for the purpose of giving concerts, commercial exchanges, such as the Metal Exchange, are created for the purpose of trade in various commodities. No one would think of defining these organisations in

[9] p. 190: " The State is a political organisation because it is an order regulating the use of force, because it monopolises the use of force."

terms of structure. I believe that the same is true of the State.

The purpose of the society which we call a State is to maintain peace and order within a demarcated territory.[10] It would be impossible to maintain a social life above the bare minimum without an organisation which prevents the arbitrary use of force by one person against another. It is only when order has been established that further progress in civilisation can be achieved. Aristotle expressed this when he said that the State begins by making life possible and then seeks to make it good. The minimum and essential purpose of the State is, therefore, to make life possible. It is, of course, true that States do not limit themselves to this minimum, but nevertheless it is this which distinguishes them from all other societies. The order which the State must aim to provide is physical order, although at various times States have also attempted to introduce other types of order. Thus, until comparatively recently, many States attempted to introduce religious order by requiring their members to belong to a particular religion. Today all States are concerned in varying degrees with the introduction of economic order, having recognised that the laissez faire doctrine of complete freedom in this field is unworkable. But it is still the maintenance of physical order which is the primary function of the State.

---

[10] *Cf.* Brierly, *The Law of Nations*, 4th ed., p. 111: " A State is an *institution*, that is to say, it is a system of relations which men establish among themselves as a means of securing certain objects, of which the most fundamental is a system of order within which their activities can be carried on."

Like all other societies the State, if it is to exist, must have rules of conduct which are directed to the achievement of this purpose. A society, although we tend to personify it, is nothing more than an organisation of men directed to a particular end. Cicero first expressed this when he said that the State was a *vinculum juris*—a legal bond between its members.[11] If this legal bond which creates the State is broken then the State comes to an end.

It follows from this that the basic law or norm, to use Kelsen's phrase, which creates the State cannot itself be created by the State. The State cannot therefore be substituted for the defunct Austinian sovereign as the source of State law. In Chapter 1 of his three-volume work on *The Law and Custom of the Constitution* [12] Sir William Anson said that when " the State defines the rules of conduct which it will enforce, and employs a uniform constraint for their enforcement—regular judicial process backed by the strong arm of the executive—it creates the Law with which alone the jurist can profitably deal." This must be one of the most remarkable definitions in all legal literature for, after stating that it is the State which makes the law, Anson devotes most of the remaining part of his work to showing that so far as constitutional law is concerned it is the law which has created the State. In his definition he speaks of the State as if it were a living material person capable of itself establishing the law, but thereafter he shows that the State is a system of government under which power is

[11] *De Re Publica* I. xxxii. 49.
[12] First published 1886–92, 5th ed., Vol. I, p. 20.

allocated to various separate bodies such as the Crown, the Houses of Parliament, and the judiciary. It is the law which tells us what these different bodies can do: it is not they who have created the constitutional law on which their power is based.

State law is therefore composed of two separate and distinct bodies of rules. The first consists in what has been well called constitutional law, for this law constitutes the State. It allocates, as I have said, to various persons and bodies the power to act within certain limits in the name of the artificial person known as the State. The second body of rules, which may be described as the constitution in action, consists in the rules established by those authorised to act by the constitutional law. The second body of rules cannot exist until the first body has been created. It is for this reason that I believe that any theory of law which ignores the first body and concentrates merely on the second is meaningless for all practical purposes.

When we turn to constitutional law it is obvious that these basic rules need not be recognised as obligatory by all persons living within the territory. There will always be a certain number of anarchists living in every society who will deny that anyone is entitled to exercise authority over them. To be effective, constitutional law must be recognised as obligatory by those who will thereby be capable of maintaining order within the territory. In certain circumstances these persons will constitute only a small proportion of the inhabitants. But even in this case it is worth repeating here that the constitutional law which those in power recognise is not based on force, but on the fact of their recognition. With the exception of exceedingly rare tyrannies we find that in almost every State the constitution is recognised as obligatory by the vast majority of the people.[13] This does not mean that they need necessarily approve actively of the constitution, or that they should base their recognition on clear grounds of reason. All that is necessary is the recognition that those who purport to exercise authority in the name of the State are authorised to do so. There is all the difference, as I have said, between obeying the order of a police officer who is recognised to have the authority of the State behind him, and the arbitrary order of a person who is merely exercising brute force. To ignore the existence of this recognition as the major element in all political life is to ignore the major fact on which society is based. I am not concerned here with the question whether a person may recognise this authority on grounds of morality, or reason, or habit. It is the existence of the recognition, and not the reason for the recognition, which is of importance. This does not mean, of course, that the people are consciously willing the existence of the constitution. On this point Professor Hagërström has said [14]:

" But it is equally incorrect to say that it was the people's will which gave to the whole system its

---

[13] Hägerström, p. 35 : " But where pure despotism or mob-rule exists one may question whether there really is any legal order. At any rate, that is not the case if legal order includes security for established rights. Yet it is pure despotism which serves as a model for the theory under discussion."

[14] p. 60.

power. For the people itself was governed by the idea in question. The whole notion of a popular resolve to maintain this idea is as absurd as to suppose that a prevalent moral climate of opinion depends on a popular resolve to maintain it."

If I am right in my conclusion that the constitution of a State consists of those recognised rules which define the exercise of power, then it is obvious that no State need have unlimited power or the monopoly of force. Our legal theory will then accord with the actual facts because we know that all States are to a certain extent limited in the exercise of power. Professor MacIver has said [15]:

" We have arrived at the days when the sovereign power, the maker of laws, the government, is told what it may do. It is so instructed in the constitutions of nearly every modern State. In these States explicitly, in all States implicitly, there are many things which are forbidden to any or all organised authorities. The limits of sovereign power are particularly marked in Federal States . . . it (the fundamental law) is superior because it is constitutive of the State itself."

It is impossible to explain the Federal system which exists in the United States, Canada and Australia under any doctrine which gives unlimited power to the State. If we take the United States as an example we find that certain powers concerning the maintenance of international peace and of inter-State order are vested in the National Government,

[15] *The Modern State*, 1926, p. 487.

while the maintenance of internal peace and order is vested in the several States. There is no difficulty here in holding that both the National and the State Governments are supreme within their own spheres, and that they can both function within the same territory. In case of a conflict between the National Government and the States concerning the exercise of their respective functions, the dispute, which arises exceedingly rarely, is referred for decision to the Supreme Court. This does not mean that the Supreme Court is a supreme Government to which the other two are subject, because its only function is to state the law as it sees it. The Supreme Court has no legislative and no executive functions: having declared the law it cannot itself do anything to see that it is enforced. The possibility of such a division of power had been denied by most political philosophers before the American Constitution came into force in 1789, and even today some European scholars have a feeling that it really cannot be true. This is due to the fact that it is difficult for those brought up in a unitary State to realise that a State need not be all-powerful and uncontrolled.

It is necessary, however, to comprehend this if we are to explain the relation between State law and moral law. If we regard State law as necessarily supreme and unlimited then any attempt to limit that power on moral grounds must fail. Under such a theory the rulers of the State may feel that they ought not to infringe certain moral principles, but this is a matter of discretion and not of law. On the other hand, if we recognise that the State is a society to which certain indefinite, but not unlimited, powers are attributed, then there is no difficulty in holding that the exercise of State power can be limited. I think that this will be recognised as a truism by most persons living in a Federal State, but it is far more difficult to suggest that such limitations are possible when we deal with a unitary State. In the case of Great Britain it is almost universally said that the Queen-in-Parliament is supreme, and that no limitations on the power of that body can be recognised. I believe that this statement is nearly as misleading as is the statement that the Queen's consent is necessary to a valid Act of Parliament. We all know that anyone who would attribute to the sovereign the power of withholding such consent would show a complete misunderstanding of the Constitution in action. In the same way I believe that whatever the theoretical power of the Queen-in-Parliament may be, there are certain general principles which are so firmly recognised as authoritative that they could not now be violated without causing a revolution. In those circumstances it seems to me to be correct to say that these principles are part of the British constitutional law. Professor Dicey in his classic work on *The Law of the Constitution* [16] has said: " The one fundamental dogma of English constitutional law is the absolute legislative sovereignty or despotism of the King-in-Parliament." This statement is, of course, perfectly true when we are discussing the question whether or not the courts can refuse to recognise a statute enacted by the Queen-in-Parliament

[16] 9th ed., 1952, p. 145.

on the ground that it is in conflict with " common right and reason." In the past a contrary view was expressed by Sir Edward Coke in *Bonham's Case*,[17] with what Sir Frederick Pollock has called [18] " his usual vehemence and even more than his usual inaccuracy or disingenuousness." The same view was expressed by Sir William Blackstone in his *Commentaries*,[19] when he stated that an Act of Parliament contrary to the law of nature would be of no validity. Today it is clear that no one would accept the views expressed by Coke [20] and Blackstone. It does not follow from this, however, that we need regard parliamentary government as a type of absolute despotism. Such a conclusion must be in conflict not only with our sense of what is fitting, but also with our recognition of what happens in fact. The answer is, I believe, that the people as a whole, and Parliament itself, recognise that under the unwritten Constitution there are certain established principles which limit the scope of Parliament. It is true that the courts cannot enforce these principles as they can under the Federal system in the United States, but this does not mean that these principles are any the less binding and effective. For that matter some of them receive greater protection today in England than they do in the United States. These basic principles are, I believe, four in number.

[17] 8 Rep. 118A.
[18] *Jurisprudence*, p. 262.
[19] Chap. 1, p. 41.
[20] Whether there ever was any truth in Coke's statement is a disputed question. On this point, Professor McIlwain and Professor Plucknett are in disagreement. The various arguments can be found in Plucknett's *History*, p. 319.

The first and most fundamental one is that no man is above the law. In the thirteenth century Henry of Bracton in his famous book *De Legibus et Consuetudinibus Angliae* said [21]:

> " The King himself ought not to be subject to any man, but he ought to be subject to God and the law, since law makes the King. Therefore let the King render to the law what the law has rendered to the King, *viz.*, dominion and power for there is no King where will rules and not the law."

As Professor Maitland has pointed out,[22] if this view had not been accepted in the thirteenth century the English kingship must have become an absolute monarchy. The same view was expressed in 1607 by Sir Edward Coke, the greatest of all Chief Justices, when he told King James that he must administer justice " according to the law and custom of England." [23] This principle is so firmly established as a part of English constitutional law that it is unthinkable that Parliament would grant such arbitrary powers to the officers of the State as would bring them above the law. It is here that the basic distinction between a totalitarian State and a constitutional State such as Great Britain can be seen. More than two thousand years ago Aristotle pointed out that the essence of constitutional law lies in the fact that it governs the magistrates who enforce it.[24] It is because the officers of the State are controlled by

[21] f. 5b.
[22] Pollock and Maitland, *History of English Law*, Vol. 1, 182.
[23] *Prohibitions Del Roy*, 12 Rep. 63.
[24] *Politics*, Bk. IV.

the law that we have democratic government instead of tyranny. It is true, of course, as I pointed out in my first lecture, that those in power in Russia recognise that law is necessary if a society is to function, but—and it is this *but* which is the all-essential thing—there are officers of the Russian State who are not controlled by this law, and who wield that absolute power which, as Lord Acton has said, tends to corrupt absolutely. If in any nation there is a group of men who are capable of disregarding the established law then we can say that here there is a tyranny. It is for this reason that such a writ as the writ of Habeas Corpus is of such fundamental importance, and has always been of such importance, in establishing liberty.[25] If any man in this country could arbitrarily imprison another man and refuse to justify the imprisonment to the courts, then we should have lost the freedom which is part of our national life. It is true, of course, that in a time of terrible national emergency, such as during the late war after the fall of France, the writ of Habeas Corpus may be temporarily suspended, but even at such a time the suspension is of only a strictly limited nature. It is, I am convinced, inconceivable that any Parliament in Great Britain would, during the ordinary conditions of peace, regard itself as constitutionally capable of abolishing the writ of Habeas Corpus. It is therefore correct to say that it is a basic part of English constitutional law that no man is above the law.

[25] *Cf.* Sir Alfred Denning, *Freedom Under the Law*, 1949, Stevens & Sons, Ltd., p. 6.

The second fundamental principle of the British Constitution is that those who govern Great Britain do so in a representative capacity and are subject to change. The elections that are held are not a meaningless ritual. It is true that at a time of great emergency Parliament is capable of continuing its own life from year to year, but if it attempted to do so indefinitely in the time of peace we should all recognise that the Constitution had been destroyed. An immortal government tends to be an immoral government, for it deprives men of that freedom of choice on which free government is based. Professor Fuller, of Harvard, has stated this truth with admirable clarity [26]:

> "The greatness of what we call democratic government does not lie in the mere fact that a numerical majority controls at election time, but at a point further removed from the ballot box, in the forces which are permitted to play upon the electorate. For in the world as it is now constituted, it is only in a democratic and constitutionally organised State that ideas have a chance to make their influence felt. By preserving a fluidity in the power structures of society, by making possible the peaceful liquidation of unsuccessful governments, democracy creates a field in which ideas may effectively compete with one another for the possession of men's minds."

Here, again, it is true to say that the free election of the members of the House of Commons is a basic

[26] *The Law in Quest of Itself*, p. 123.

principle of English constitutional law. Without "the peaceful liquidation of unsuccessful governments" the English system would come to an end.

The third basic principle covers the so-called freedoms of speech, of thought and of assembly. These freedoms are an essential part of any Constitution which provides that the people shall be free to govern themselves, because without them self-government becomes impossible. A totalitarian government, which claims to have absolute and unalterable authority, is acting in a logical manner if it denies to its subjects the right of criticism, because such criticism may affect the authority of those in power. To ask that a totalitarian government should recognise freedom of speech is to ask for the impossible because, by its very nature, such a government must limit the freedom of its subjects. On the other hand, such a system of government as exists under the British Constitution must recognise the necessity for freedom of speech and of association, because if public criticism is forbidden and if men are prevented from acting together in political associations, then it would be impossible to make a change in the government by the free, and more or less intelligent, choice of the people.

This does not mean that the constitutional government of a State must recognise that there is a right to advocate the overthrow of that constitution by force, because force is the negation of reason. You cannot argue safely with a man who is threatening to draw a revolver. Like all the rights which the law gives, the liberty which a man has to express his

opinions is not an absolute one, but must be exercised within reasonable bounds. It is one of the virtues of the common law that it refuses to go to extremes; the argument that because the law has taken step A therefore it is logical that it should also take the further step B has never impressed the English judges. Having spent little time in the study of metaphysics, they have not been misled by this specious argument. It is because the common-law rights of the English-man are never doctrinaire that they have such strength and vitality. Here, again, it is obvious that Parliament could not, even if it wished to do so, abolish freedom of speech in this country. It is there-fore correct, both in fact and in theory, to say that this limitation is a part of constitutional law.

The fourth and final principle which is a basic part of the English constitution is the independence of the judiciary. It would be inconceivable that Parliament should today regard itself as free to abolish the principle which has been accepted as a corner-stone of freedom ever since the Act of Settlement in 1701. It has been recognised as axiomatic that if the judiciary were placed under the authority of either the legisla-tive or the executive branches of the Government then the administration of the law might no longer have that impartiality which is essential if justice is to prevail.

It is important to point out that the doctrine establishing the independence of the judiciary does not mean that the judges themselves are absolute. They are bound to follow the law which they administer.[27] To deny that the judges are subject to the law, because there may be no effective sanction if they disregard it, is to misunderstand the nature of law itself. The judges recognise that they are bound by the law, just as the army recognises that it is bound by the law. If either group refused to obey we would, of course, have a revolution. The only difference between the two would be that the military revolution would be more likely to succeed than the judicial one.

It is therefore, I believe, true to say that it is as wrong in theory as it is in fact to suggest that the British Constitution is a form of enlightened despotism. Those who exercise power in the name of the State are bound by the law, and there are certain definite principles which limit the exercise of that power. It has been suggested that the basic principles which I have set forth would gain greater protection if the Constitution were in written form, and if these principles were set out in a separate Bill of Rights such as is found in the American Constitution. I doubt whether this would prove to be of any practical advantage, except perhaps to the lawyers, because these principles will find adequate protection so long as democratic government exists, and they will

[27] It is for this reason that I regard the theory of the administration of justice as taught by the American realists as misleading. They give the impression that the judges have a freedom which, if exercised, would be the negation of law. On the other hand, I believe that Judge Jerome Frank has made a useful contribution in his emphasis on the fact that law cannot be found in the written word only. It depends on recognition, and in certain instances it may be difficult to foretell the course that this will take.

disappear if absolute government takes its place, whether they are written on a piece of paper or not. It is the conviction, ingrained in the average Englishman by tradition and by education, that it is his moral duty to be free which is the only certain guarantee against arbitrary government.

We find, therefore, that constitutional law and moral law are closely interwoven. This constitutional law cannot depend on any sanction; it is founded on the recognition, both on the part of those in power and of those subject to the power, that there is an obligation to obey the rules which constitute the State. This sense of obligation is in great part a moral one, and any attempt to deny this fact will lead us to a misunderstanding of history. It is because this sense of obligation is founded in part on the moral law that revolutions when they come are frequently an expression of a clash of moral ideas. This is true in particular of the history of Great Britain and of those nations which have sprung from her, for our revolutions have been fought on questions of principle. The constitution as it exists today is more firmly based than ever in the past, for the rules in which that constitution is expressed are in accord, on all substantial points, with the moral law as recognised by the people of this country.

ADMINISTRATIVE LAW

Perhaps no subject has been more controversial in recent years than has administrative law. So much has been written on this topic that one feels that even a brief reference to it requires an apology.[28]

There are some authorities who regard the phrase " administrative law " as a misnomer. They argue that regulations which are issued by Ministers and which are thereafter enforced by administrative tribunals lack the nature of law. There can be no law, they say, unless it is enforced by the judges. This was the theme of Lord Hewart's often-quoted book *The New Despotism*.[29] I do not agree with this view because it is in direct conflict with my interpretation of law. If law consists of rules which are recognised as obligatory, then there can be no ground on which the character of law can be denied to those rules which are recognised as obligatory by administrative tribunals. There is no magic in the fact that one tribunal is called judicial and another administrative, provided that both of them are governed by obligatory rules. The distinction between them lies in the fact that far more discretion is usually given to the administrative tribunal than is given to a court of law. From my personal experience I know that an administrative tribunal has little difficulty in distinguishing between those of its decisions which are made under the law, *viz.*, in accordance with fixed rules, and those which are based on its discretionary powers. This distinction, which is of the greatest practical importance, cannot be adequately appreciated if we fail to understand the nature of law.

---

[28] Perhaps I may refer in particular to the contributions made by Sir Cecil Carr, Sir Carleton Allen, Sir Ivor Jennings, Professor E. C. S. Wade, and Professor Robson.

[29] 1929.

The two main criticisms of administrative law as it exists at the present time are both moral in character. The first concerns what may be termed the incognisability of administrative law. It is obviously wrong that a man should be bound by rules of whose existence he cannot know. The fact that the Emperor Caligula placed his decrees on the top of a monument, where they could not be read, has not endeared him either to the jurist or the moralist. The force of this criticism has received increasing recognition in recent years with the result that some of the injustices to which Sir Carleton Allen called attention in his book *Law and Orders* [30] are unlikely to recur.

The second criticism of administrative law is a graver one, and one which it is more difficult to meet —it is that administrative tribunals may fail to do what has been called " natural justice." They must give the interested party a fair hearing, but it is not at all clear what constitutes fairness. Must he be given an opportunity to see and reply to all the evidence which the tribunal has received? On this point it is difficult to reconcile *Arlidge's Case* [31] with *Errington's Case*.[32] The major difficulty is that no uniform method of procedure is followed by the various tribunals. On this point Allen has said [33]: " Thus, while we now have a large number of tribunals deciding questions of great importance to the citizen,

[30] 1945.
[31] *Local Government Board* v. *Arlidge* [1915] A.C. 120.
[32] *Errington* v. *Minister of Health* [1935] 1 K.B. 249.
[33] *Law in the Making*, 5th ed., p. 575.

there is no consistency in the procedure by which they work; and some of them, like the Furnished Rents Tribunals, seem to have no defined procedure at all." The remedy that has been suggested for this unsatisfactory state of affairs is the creation of some appellate system not unlike that in force in France as part of the droit administratif. There may be objections to the particular schemes that have been advanced, but sooner or later some procedure along these lines will have to be adopted, because it can be satisfactory neither from the moral nor the legal standpoint that there should be a considerable number of persons who feel that they have been denied under the laws of the country what they regard as natural justice. If a philosopher attempts to explain to them that there is no such thing as natural justice their reply will be uncomplimentary.

INTERNATIONAL LAW

In English constitutional law we find a legal system which is in accord with and firmly based on moral law. When we turn to international law we find an illustration of the truth that a legal system, however complete in theory, may be totally ineffective if there is no recognised moral law which will give it adequate support. It has been said that international law is weak because there is no sovereign body to command it, and it is also argued that it is the absence of adequate legal machinery which has prevented the development of this law. I do not believe that there is any truth in either of these arguments.[34] The weakness of international law is due to the absence of an international moral sense. In regard to constitutional law we find in this country an overwhelming conviction that the rules of the Constitution must be obeyed: on the other hand, in regard to international law, we tend to find a general belief in most countries that there is no serious obligation to obey those rules if they are in conflict with the national interest.

As a result there are many thoughtful men who hold that there is in fact no such thing as international law. Perhaps the most extraordinary example of this can be found in the statement made by Sir Thomas Holland [35]:

> " Convenient therefore as is on many accounts the phrase ' International Law,' to express those rules of conduct in accordance with which, either in consequence of their express consent, or in pursuance of the usage of the civilised world, nations are expected to act, it is impossible to regard these rules as being in reality anything more than the moral code of nations."

It is difficult to believe that the author of this statement was the Chichele Professor of International Law in the University of Oxford, and President of the Institut de Droit International. It must be rare, indeed, to find a professor who alleges that the subject which he purports to profess does not exist.

---

[34] I have discussed these in *Transactions of the Grotius Society* (1936) xxii, 33.
[35] *Jurisprudence*, 13th ed., p. 135.

Holland was forced to reach this conclusion because, being an Austinian, he defined law as a command. In the international community of States there obviously is no sovereign authority which can give commands to the free and independent States, and there is no sanction if they arbitrarily break the rules which the international community is supposed to recognise as obligatory.[36] The result of this view is that what is universally called international law is nothing more than convention, supported in part by custom and in part by agreement. If this were merely a matter of nomenclature it would not be of great importance, although the Emperor Augustus was right when he said that men are frequently ruled by words, but the disbelief in the existence of international law may destroy not only its efficacy but its very existence, because if it lacks legal validity then there is little reason why a State should obey it when it is to its advantage not to do so. The views expressed by many German legal philosophers that international law was purely consensual in character and had no binding force on the nations of the world, undoubtedly

---

[36] Professor Oppenheim purported to find a sanction in the so-called right of self-help. Similarly, Professor Kelsen finds it in war and reprisals. A sanction which gives Holland the right of self-help against Germany seems to be more formal than realistic. On this point Allen has said (*Law in the Making*, p. 55): " History does not tell us of any society in which self-help has been a legal sanction in and of itself— that is, without reference to some higher authority, which ultimately will reinforce the individual's own means of redress. Indeed, a society in which self-help was the sole ' legal ' sanction would not be a society in any recognisable sense of the term, but merely an animal condition of anarchy."

encouraged the rulers of that country in their disregard of its provisions.[37]

Fortunately for international law in this country, the force interpretations of law have never achieved general acceptance here. The English courts have for many centuries held that international law is an obligatory body of rules which the members of the society of nations must recognise. This does not mean that the English courts have the power under the Constitution to disregard an English statute which they may hold is in conflict with international law, but, in the absence of such overriding authority, they have held that international law must be recognised by them and that it therefore forms a part of English law. In 1775 in *Barbuit's Case*,[38] Lord Chancellor Talbot said: " The law of nations in its fullest extent is and forms part of the law of England." In *Chung Chi Cheung* v. *The King*,[39] the famous piracy case, Lord Atkin, in delivering the judgment of the Privy Council, said: " The courts acknowledge the existence of a body of rules which nations accept among themselves. On any judicial issue they seek to ascertain what the relevant rule is, and, having found it, they will treat it as incorporated into the domestic law." It would be possible to continue almost indefinitely the quotations from judgments in which the courts

[37] *Cf.* Brierly, p. 54: " Most of these [German] writers admit that a self-imposed limitation is no limitation at all; and they conclude, therefore, that so-called international law is nothing but ' external public law ' (*äusseres Staatsrecht*), binding the State only because, and only so long as, it consents to be bound."

[38] Cas.t.Talbot 281.

[39] [1939] A.C. 160.

have recognised that international law consists in a recognised body of rules which has been incorporated into English law. This doctrine is based on the view that these rules have been recognised and are accepted as being obligatory.

Why have these rules of international law been recognised as obligatory even though obedience to them by the various nations has at best been only spasmodic? Before the seventeenth century they were regarded as part of the law of God which reasonable men could discover in the basic principles of the Christian religion. Perhaps the noblest expression of this view can be found in the books of the great Spanish Catholic jurists Vitoria and Suarez. This religious law of nature and of nations became, however, less effective in the seventeenth century with the break between the Catholic and the Protestant Churches. A new foundation had to be established which could be accepted by those who held conflicting religious views, and it was found by Grotius in a law of nature based on pure reason. This law was regarded as so fundamental that it was binding even on God himself. On this law of nature the rules of international law were based. Treaties were binding because it was a law of nature that promises must be kept: *pacta sunt servanda* was the rock on which all agreements were founded. Cruelty to the civilian population was illegal because it was against reason that innocent persons should be killed or tortured. International law was obligatory because all reasonable men must recognise that it received its validity from eternal moral principles. It was not, however, completely coincident with the moral law because one of its necessary elements consisted in general recognition by the civilised States of the world. This concept of international law was summarised by Lord Mansfield in these words [40]: " The law of nations is founded on justice, equity, convenience, and the reason of the thing, and confirmed by long usage."

I believe that international law today is still based, in Professor Brierly's words,[41] on " the moral foundation which is essential to the vitality of all legal obligation," but the difficulty is that the people of the world do not sufficiently recognise the nature of this moral foundation. In the case of the rules which prohibit the murder of prisoners of war and of the civilian population this foundation is obvious, but what have morals to do, it may be asked, with the more technical rules of international law? The answer is, I believe, that we can never be freed from the scourge of war until we establish a strong international community, and that that community cannot be strong until we recognise that no society can exist if its rules are disregarded. If each State is regarded as unbound by any duties to the others, then there can be little hope for any advance in our civilisation. We must then live in a Hobbesian world in which each nation is the natural enemy of its neighbours, and aggressive war, instead of being the greatest of all crimes, is merely regarded as an instrument of policy. If we are to avoid this result we must recognise that there is a community of nations bound

[40] Cited by Pollock, *Essays in the Law*, p. 64.
[41] p. 45.

together by definite rules, and that there is a moral obligation to obey them because if they are disregarded then the international society will collapse.

International law, like every other legal system, depends therefore on recognition. The weakness of international law at the present time is not due to the inadequacy of its rules or to the incompetence of the international lawyers. It is due to a moral weakness in the world itself. Until the nations of the world pay more than lip service to these rules, and as long as they are prepared to break them whenever it is to their immediate advantage, these rules will continue to be feeble and ineffective. I think that it can be a matter for just pride in this country that when we study the history of international law it is clear that no other nation in the world has been more ready to recognise and to obey the authority of these rules than has Great Britain, although no one could claim that there have not been occasions when even this country has violated them. By and large, however, obedience has been the rule, not because of the fear of any sanction, but because of the conviction that there was a moral duty to obey. It is therefore, I believe, true to say that the relationship between international law and the moral law is the foundation on which international law, as recognised by the English courts, is based.

CRIMINAL LAW, TORTS
AND CONTRACT

3

CRIMINAL LAW, TORTS AND CONTRACT

BEFORE discussing the influence of moral law on the particular branches of English law, I must say a few words concerning the points of contact between the civil and the moral law. Professor Roscoe Pound has dealt with this question in such detail in his essay *Law and Morals*,[1] that it is not necessary for me to discuss it here at any length. It is, however, important to distinguish the different occasions on which this relationship is particularly marked.

The first, and most obvious, point of contact between the civil and moral law is when the civil law is being made. The legislator who is concerned with some new statute will, in many cases, take into consideration the moral law both because he feels that he himself is bound by the moral law, and also because, as a practical politician, he must realise that a statute which conflicts with the moral law, as recognised by the people of this country, will find it difficult to survive. There are, of course, large parts of the civil law in which no moral question arises because the problem is purely a practical one. The Wills Act, 1837, is an obvious instance. There can be no moral question in regard to the provision that a will must be signed by the testator in the presence of two witnesses who must each sign in each other's presence. The

[1] 1924, Oxford University Press.

question here whether one, two or three witnesses
should be required is clearly a practical one. On the
other hand, the various provisions of the law concerning inheritance are largely concerned with moral
questions. There is first of all the question whether
property ought to be inheritable at all. Then there
is the question whether the present holder of property
ought to be entitled to say what is to be its destination
after his death; thus it has been argued that the
English law, which gives almost complete power to the
testator, is in conflict with morality because it allows
the dead hand to govern the living. Again the
question whether a father should be entitled arbitrarily
to disinherit his children is in large part a moral one.
The influence of the moral law on legislation is, however, so self-evident that it is unnecessary to elaborate
the point here.

Law-making is not, however, limited to the legislature. Today we all recognise that the judges have
certain law-making powers, and that this is inevitable,
however detailed a code or a statute on the subject
may be. No legislator is ever omniscient. The law-
making powers of the judges are, however, more
restricted than are those of the legislature because, as
Mr. Justice Holmes has said,[2] they can only legislate
" interstitially." A judge obviously cannot disregard
a statute, however much he may regard it as being in
conflict with contemporary morals. He can, however,
interpret it strictly so that its effect is as limited as
possible. One illustration of this is the famous or

[2] *Southern Pacific Co.* v. *Jensen*, 244 U.S. 205, 221.

infamous Statute of Frauds,[3] which has been judicially described as a statute for frauds. The judges have, whenever possible, restricted its scope. Similarly the Sunday Observance Act [4] is in many ways obsolete today and in conflict with the general moral standards of the country, but here again the judges are not free to disregard it.

English judges are also restricted by the rule that a judge is bound by a precedent if it is directly in point. The English doctrine is stricter than that followed in most other countries because it is based on the binding nature of a single case.[5] The question whether the English doctrine is a desirable one has given rise in recent years to a considerable literature. Like most other difficult problems, it represents in part a conflict between opposing moral ideas. Those in favour of the strict doctrine base it on the desire for certainty in the law.[6] Apart from its practical advantages, this

---

[3] 1677, 29 Car. 2, c. iii. Of this statute Sir William Holdsworth (*History of English Law*, Vol. VI, p. 396) has said: " The prevailing feeling both in the legal and the commercial world is, and has for a long time been, that these clauses have outlived their usefulness, and are quite out of place amid the changed legal and commercial conditions of today." *Cf.* note in (1927) 43 L.Q.R. 1.

[4] 1677, 29 Car. 2, c. 7, s. 1.

[5] This is discussed at length in my *Precedent in English and Continental Law*. 1934. Stevens & Sons, Ltd. Perhaps the best presentation of the various aspects of this difficult problem can be found in Professor Paton's *Jurisprudence*, 2nd ed., 1951, s. 44.

[6] In his Presidential Address to the Holdsworth Club on *The Limits of Precedent* (1943) Viscount Simon said: " To those who find it astonishing that the House of Lords, sitting judicially, should reaffirm a proposition of law that later argument might show to be wrong, there are two answers. First, when the House of Lords has once laid down the proposition, it is no longer wrong: it is the law and everybody

certainty expresses the moral view that men should be able to plan their acts with a clear understanding concerning their legal consequences. If these are uncertain then men may be held liable without sufficient warning. Again certainty in precedents may guarantee equality, which is a moral concept, for if A's case is decided in one way today it is right that B's case, based on similar facts, should be decided in the same way tomorrow. No one will dispute the force of these arguments, but perhaps certainty can be bought at too high a price. There is not much to be said, as Lord Wright has expressed it,[7] for the certainty of injustice. There is little danger that a less strict rule would lead to revolutionary measures because the law by its very nature tends to be conservative. It can, therefore, be argued that judges ought not to be forced to follow a precedent when it is clear that the moral law to which it originally gave expression has fundamentally changed.[8] It may be

should proceed on that footing. And secondly, the cure for these difficulties, if cure is needed, is by legislation which amends the decision by putting a different statutory provision in its place." Perhaps it may be suggested that although a judgment delivered by the House of Lords cannot be wrong, nevertheless it may be highly inconvenient, especially if the social and economic conditions have altered in the intervening years. Nor is it easy to alter the law by legislation because the Parliamentary programme is always overcrowded.

[7] (1943) 8 Camb.L.J. 118; (1950) 13 Mod.L.R. 23.

[8] The greatest of English legal historians, Frederick Maitland, has said (*Collected Papers* iii, 486–7):

"For myself, I happen to think that legal history is a fascinating matter for study. It is pleasant, and I even believe that it is profitable, to trace the origins of legal rules in the social and economic conditions of a bygone age. But anyone who really possesses what has been called the historic sense must, so it seems to me, dislike to see a rule said, however, that the bark of the English doctrine is worse than its bite, because when the judges are convinced that a precedent ought not to be followed then they frequently succeed in " distinguishing " it out of existence.

With these limitations in mind, it is clear that the judges do make law in three ways. The first is when there is no existing law on the subject. Perhaps the best illustration of this can be found in the law relating to aeroplanes. Before it was possible to enact any statutes on this subject, it was necessary, especially in the United States, for the courts to consider the nature of the liability incurred by a man whose plane had been involved in an accident. Ought he to be held strictly liable for all damage on the basis that he had created a peculiar risk, or ought this liability be limited to negligence on his part? It is clear that in deciding such a question the judges would be influenced by their views concerning moral responsibility, *i.e.*, to what extent is it right that one man may place the risk of harmful consequences arising from his acts on another? These cases of " first impression " are, however, comparatively rare, and there are even some authorities who deny that they can ever arise, on the ground that there is always some general principle under which they can be subsumed.

or an idea unfitly surviving in a changed environment. An anachronism should offend not only his reason, but his taste.''
In his lecture on *The Work of the Court of Appeal* Sir Raymond Evershed, Master of the Rolls, cited this passage.

The second and far more frequent instance of judicial law-making arises when there is a choice between conflicting laws, or between conflicting precedents. They may be said to be conflicting in the sense that each is equally applicable to the circumstances under consideration. In making such a choice the judge may be influenced by moral considerations.[9] This may be a difficult problem because a judge must always remember that in making his choice he is establishing a precedent for the future, and that what may be moral in the peculiar circumstances of the case he is considering may turn out to have an opposite result in other cases.

The third method of judicial law-making is found in the interpretation of statutes. This has become a matter of increasing concern at the present time because of the flood of legislation, especially of delegated legislation called statutory instruments. The conflict between the grammatical method of interpretation and what has been described as the liberal method is too well known to need elaboration here. To whichever method the judge may pay lip service, I think that it is clear that he will almost inevitably be influenced by moral considerations in his interpretation, because, if given a choice, it is unlikely that a judge will choose an interpretation which he thinks will lead to an undesirable result. There is always the presumption that Parliament, and even Ministers, have intended to act in a reasonable manner. The judge may rely on

---

[9] The nature of this choice was discussed by Judge Cardozo in *The Nature of the Judicial Process*, 1921, and *The Growth of the Law*, 1923.

the literal interpretation when he desires one result, and on the liberal approach when he desires another.

It is therefore correct to say that in all the three methods of law-making which I have outlined the judges may be influenced by the moral law. But what moral law are we talking about here? Is it the moral law as seen by the judge himself, or the moral law as it is regarded by the community in general? I do not think that it is possible to give a clear-cut answer. In certain cases the judges have undoubtedly accepted a standard of morality which is above the general average. An example of this can be found in the law relating to the duties of a trustee, which have become so strict that it has been found necessary to give the trustee some protection by legislation.[10] On the other hand, it is clear that a judge who is a convinced pro-hibitionist will not attempt to translate his moral views into law. What can be said with confidence is that the English judges have rarely attempted to deal with this problem on general philosophical grounds; thus, when we turn to the law of tort we shall see that they have never established any general theory such as " no liability without fault." Professor Winfield has summed up his researches on this point in these words [11] :

> " There is not the faintest trace in current English case law of any attempt on the part of the judges to make the law conform to any ideal ethical standard. Where there is any scope for the

[10] Trustee Act, 1925.
[11] *Essays on Tort*, 1953, p. 285.

application of morals to the law, what they do apply is the practical morality which is prevalent for the time being in the community."

Turning from judicial legislation we find that the third point of contact between law and morals is found in the application of certain legal terms which contain in themselves a moral element. The most important of these in English law is the term " reasonable." The reasonable man, as we all know, is the hero of the English law. It is he who furnishes the yard stick by which the conduct of the ordinary man must, in many instances, be measured. But the reasonable man is not only the prudent and sensible man, he is also the moral man. It is reasonable for him to act in accord with the proper moral standards, and so his actions are both controlled by morals and can be used as a test for morals. There are, as Professor Winfield has pointed out,[12] other legal terms such as " fair," " malice," and " just," which connote moral ideas, but they are less important than the basic idea of reasonableness. In the past the application of these standards was left in large part to the jury in civil cases, but with the virtual disappearance of the jury these standards must now be applied by the judges who try the cases. It will be interesting to see whether this will have any effect in altering the standards themselves.

Finally, we find a contact between law and morals in those parts of the administration of justice where the judge acts partly according to law and partly

[12] *Ibid.*, p. 278.

according to discretion. All discretionary remedies come under this heading. The judge must exercise, not an arbitrary, but an informed discretion, and in doing so he may turn to moral rules as a guide. This may be illustrated by the case in which specific performance of a contract may be granted or refused. Although the contract may be a perfectly valid one, enforceable at common law, the court may refuse such a decree if it reaches the conclusion that it would be unjust to do so on the ground that the promisee had taken an unfair advantage of the promisor. The best illustration of judicial discretion is found, however, in the criminal law. Two centuries ago many sentences were fixed rigidly by the law with the result that the judge had little discretion in this field. Today, with the exception of treason and murder, there are no automatic sentences, and in the case of manslaughter the scale of punishment may run from life imprisonment to a small fine. What moral considerations will affect a judge in determining the nature and degree of the punishment to be awarded can be conveniently discussed as a part of criminal law which I shall now consider.

CRIMINAL LAW

When we turn to the criminal law, we find that the danger is not that we may underrate the influence of the moral law, but that we may exaggerate it. Because criminal law in its more severe aspect punishes what are generally regarded as wicked acts, we are inclined to think that the criminal law is " morality with teeth in it," and that its primary purpose must be to make men good. Any attempts to define criminal law in terms of morality have, however, failed because even such a crime as treason may not be morally wrong, and the vast majority of minor offences are unrelated to moral fault. A crime can only be defined as an act which is punished by the State.[13] What acts will be so prohibited is a question of public policy. In early law the criminal law is concerned primarily with the maintenance of physical peace and order: this is inevitable for the minimum purposes of the State are directed to this end. Therefore, it is obvious that such acts as treason, murder, robbery and rape will be regarded as criminal.[14] As the purposes of the State begin to extend so will its criminal law, especially when these purposes are directed to the well-being of its individual members. Thus acts, such as, for example, the sale of defective food, may today have criminal liability attached to them although, in the past, they constituted only civil wrongs. In most instances, however, the law will be content to allow the individual to protect his own interests by means of the civil law. Thus a breach of contract, however reprehensible it may be from the moral standpoint, will not, as a general rule, entail criminal liability, but in special cases, where a breach of contract may affect the good order of the community as a whole, as, for example, the breach of a

[13] C. S. Kenny, *Outlines of Criminal Law,* 15th ed., p. 20.
[14] It is not necessary for me to discuss here the disputed question whether in early law the law of torts preceded the criminal law. In all legal systems that have attained any degree of maturity these acts are regarded as crimes.

contract of service in an essential public service,[15] the law may regard this as a criminal offence. It is still the protection of the public welfare, rather than the support of private interests, which is the dominant purpose of this branch of the law.

The mistaken emphasis placed on the moral law in relation to crime is due in part to the maxim which, as Professor Kenny [16] has pointed out, has been familiar to English lawyers for nearly eight hundred years: " *actus non facit reum nisi mens sit rea.*" This is misleading because *mens rea* is usually defined as a wicked mind, thus implying that the law is here concerned with the moral guilt of the wrongdoer. This, however, is a misinterpretation because in most crimes *mens rea* means nothing more than that the person has intentionally done the prohibited act, and that he must realise that certain consequences are likely to follow from his conduct. Thus, a mother who kills her child to save it from a lifetime of inevitable suffering may be acting from what she regards as the highest moral motive, but her act is intentional and therefore criminal in the eyes of the law. The law is concerned solely with the fact that an act, which it has defined as criminal, has been committed: it is only in the matter of punishment that, as a general rule, moral guilt or innocence becomes relevant.

The misinterpretation of *mens rea* as a consciously wicked mind has led to what I regard as an unfortunate attitude in regard to what may be termed

---

[15] Conspiracy and Protection of Property Act, 1875, s. 4. This provision has been amended from time to time.
[16] p. 40.

crimes of negligence and crimes of absolute liability. It has been suggested that manslaughter, where the killing has been caused inadvertently, and lesser crimes of negligence involving personal injury, ought to be regarded as exceptional because the wrong-doer has not intended the consequences of his act. The law, however, is not concerned to make an analysis of the degree of moral guilt of the person who has acted negligently: it is seeking to prevent injuries to innocent third persons, and if it can only do so effectively by making harmful acts criminal then there can be no reason why it should not take this necessary step.

At first sight there seems to be greater difficulty in justifying crimes based on vicarious liability. As a general rule it must seem unreasonable to punish a man for an act, committed without his help or authorisation, by another. Here the criminal law seems to be not coincident with but in conflict with the moral law. The answer is that the criminal law is not in such a case concerned with moral guilt, but is seeking to enforce the maximum degree of care on the part of the person in authority. Various provisions of the Factory Acts, the Mines Acts, the Licensing Acts, and others of a like nature are illustrations of this. During the recent war the provisions concerning rationing and price control offences were almost all of an absolute character, because they could not have been enforced if the *mens rea* of the offenders had been a necessary element in the commission of the offence. It was the absolute duty of the shopkeeper to see that the law was obeyed, and if he failed to do so he was held criminally responsible.

The relation between the criminal law and the moral law becomes a peculiarly difficult one when we consider the criminal liability of those who are mentally defective. If we could draw a clear line between weakness of character and weakness of intellect, as our ancestors thought was possible, the problem would not be insoluble, but unfortunately we cannot take that course. The law has, I think, reached the only possible conclusion that in determining the criminal guilt of a person the only relevant question is whether he knew the nature of his act, and had the necessary *mens rea*, where this is required by the law. If an act is criminal only when the actor knows that it is unlawful, then this knowledge must be shown. Thus, in a murder case to establish the crime the only question is whether the actor knows the true nature of the act he is doing, and knows that it is morally or legally wrong. Whether he should be punished for committing this crime is an entirely different problem. Similarly, some women are driven by an irresistible impulse to steal things which are of no possible use to them so that it is clear that they are acting under a mental defect. They are found guilty of having committed the crime, but are then given mental treatment which not infrequently proves effective. It would obviously be unreasonable to punish them for an act which they could not help doing; but this does not mean that the law should not find them guilty of having done it. If the law were to attempt to draw a distinction between an irresistible impulse and one which had not been resisted it would find itself involved in a hopeless series of medical and psychological problems. Guilt can usually be determined without much difficulty, and the courts are well qualified to do this; on the other hand, moral responsibility may be an indefinite concept which is a matter of impression rather than of proof. Thus, in a shop-lifting case, the question whether the woman knowingly took the goods is a question of fact which can be proved by evidence in court: on the other hand, the question whether she should be regarded as fully responsible, and therefore subject to punishment, or, to take the other extreme, as a moral defective owing to mental causes, and therefore subject to medical treatment, is one which, at the present time, may give rise in many cases to a difference in medical opinion, and which may depend for its answer on prolonged and not always conclusive tests. Today these two entirely different questions concerning guilt and responsibility tend to be dealt with as if they constituted a single one, with the result that confusion is introduced. This is due in large part to the fact that it is usually in murder cases that the question of insanity is raised.

I believe that this confusion will continue until the law ceases to provide that anyone convicted of murder must be sentenced to be hanged.[17] The much criticised *McNaghten Rules*,[18] when applied to murder cases,

---

[17] Ralph Partridge, *Broadmoor*, 1953, discusses the distinction between legal and medical insanity in a clear and forceful manner.

[18] *R*. v. *McNaghten* (1843) 10 Cl. & F. 200.

seem to many people to be unreasonable, because they justifiably feel that it is morally wrong to hang a man who has acted under an irresistible impulse. This unreasonableness disappears to a great extent in practice, because in such a case the Home Secretary may recommend a reprieve, but no jury is ever certain that this will happen. In other words, it is the death sentence, and not the *McNaghten Rules*, which brings the law of insanity in murder cases into conflict with the moral law in many instances. It is, I believe, right that the only questions which a jury should be asked are (1) did the prisoner commit the act, (2) did he know the nature of the act he was committing, and (3) did mental disease prevent him from knowing that what he was doing was legally or morally wrong? What causes the difficulty is that the answers to these questions (affirmative to the first two and negative to the third) should lead to the automatic imposition of the death penalty. If the death penalty were abolished the various problems relating to legal insanity would, in large part, disappear also, just as they have in the case of other crimes. In saying this I am not arguing that it may not be necessary for other reasons to retain the death penalty, although I am not convinced that it is, but it is important that we should realise that part of the price we pay for the death penalty is inevitable confusion in the law relating to the legal responsibility of those who have a disease of the mind. As long as a man's life may depend on the thin and uncertain line drawn between sanity and insanity it will be impossible to administer the law in a fair and dispassionate manner. Juries will continue to find insanity in cases in which the prisoner clearly knew the nature of his or her act and knew that it was wrong—the crime of infanticide [19] had to be introduced to deal with some of these cases—if they feel that the death penalty is inappropriate, and in other cases, where their emotions are roused, the prisoner will be found sane, although from the medical standpoint he is undoubtedly suffering from a grave mental disease. [20] This introduces an element of uncertainty into the law which helps to make many murder trials exciting sporting events for the general public. When the death penalty was temporarily suspended, murder trials disappeared from the front pages of the newspapers.

In no part of the criminal law is it more important to understand the correct relationship between State law and moral law than it is in regard to punishment. If the purposes of the criminal law were to make men morally good and to punish sin then we should have to frame our theory of punishment with these ends in view, but if we remember that the primary purpose of the criminal law is the protection of the public welfare then we can use this as a touchstone in discussing this difficult problem. But even if we keep

---

[19] The Infanticide Act, 1922.
[20] The notorious Ronald True case in 1922 is an illustration of this. His family knew that he had gone mad and had a private detective searching for him to get him certified when he murdered an unfortunate girl. The jury duly brought in a verdict of guilty, but he was reprieved.

this purpose of the criminal law in mind there still will be moral questions for us to consider.

The aims of punishment have been classified as preventive, reformative, retributive and deterrent.[21] The first two give rise to few moral problems as it is obvious that it is in accord with the moral law to prevent a man from committing a crime and to reform him if he has done so. In preventive punishment, which is, in fact, a misnomer, because the prevention is used not as a punishment for a crime that has been committed but as a physical method by which the commission of another crime can be stopped, the main problem is one of degree. If a man has committed three or four larcenies it is highly probable that he will continue to do so again if he is left at liberty. Is it right in these circumstances for the State to deprive him permanently of liberty so as to protect the public welfare? The answer will depend in part on a balance between the amount of danger to the public and of suffering for the individual. On the other hand, in the case of reformative punishment the primary question is one concerning its efficacy. It must always be the hope of any rational penal system that those who are subject to it will in the future be deflected from their criminal ways. In recent years remarkable advances have been made along these lines, especially in the training of the juvenile wrongdoer, but no one, except a few

---

[21] *Cf.* Paton, *Jurisprudence*, pp. 287–305. See also J. Michael and M. J. Adler, *Crime Law and Social Science*, 1933, and A. C. Ewing, *The Morality of Punishment*, 1929.

enthusiasts, will be prepared to argue that reformation can by itself solve the problem of crime and punishment.

It is when we turn to retributive punishment that we find our most difficult moral problem. On this subject the greatest of German philosophers, Immanuel Kant, has said [22]: " The penal law is a categorical imperative; and woe to him who creeps through the serpentine windings of utilitarianism to discover some consideration which, by its promise or advantage, should free the criminal from the penalty, or even from any degree thereof." This " categorical imperative " has never made much impression upon the English law. Nor has the view that the essential equality of crime and punishment must always be established.[23] Unfortunately, these exaggerated doctrinaire statements have led to a reaction, with the result that it has become the generally accepted view that retributive punishment can never be justified. Retribution and revenge are regarded as synonymous. It must be remembered, however, that criminal law does not function in a vacuum, and that it cannot ignore the human beings with whom it has to deal. There seems to be an instinctive feeling in most ordinary men that a person who has done an injury to others should be punished for it. As civilisation develops this feeling is limited to intentional or negligent injuries, but the principle remains the same. It has, therefore, been pointed out that if the criminal law refuses to recognise retributive punishment then

[22] Kant, *The Science of Right*, Part 2, Sect. 49, E.
[23] Hegel, *Philosophy of Right*, ss. 97–104.

there is a danger that people will take the law into their own hands. A far greater danger, to my mind, is that without a sense of retribution we may lose our sense of wrong. Retribution in punishment is an expression of the community's disapproval of crime, and if this retribution is not given recognition then the disapproval may also disappear. A community which is too ready to forgive the wrongdoer may end by condoning the crime.

Finally, there is the deterrent purpose of punishment which is, to my mind, by far its most important function, because without it criminal law would lose most of its effectiveness. The criminal law deters men from committing acts of which the State disapproves by threatening them with an adequate punishment.[24] In most instances this threat is sufficient to secure the obedience of those who might otherwise be prepared to break the law. This is deterrence, pure and simple, which takes effect before a wrong has been done. It is a warning to all men of what will happen to them if they break the law.

It is more usual, however, to speak of deterrence after a crime has been committed. This may take two forms. The first is the deterrence which will keep the wrongdoer from again committing a crime. It is closely related to the reformatory purpose of punishment which is aimed at such an improvement in his character that he will not break the law again because

---

[24] It is here that the force, command, and sanction theories of law become realistic. It is for this reason that those who support these theories take their illustrations from the criminal law.

he recognises that it is wrong: in the case of deterrence he will not break the law again because he
recognises that it may be painful for him to do so.
The second and much more important form of
deterrence is the deterrence of others because of the
punishment meted out to the wrongdoer. It is here
that we come to the difficult moral problem. Those
who object to this form of deterrence argue that it can
never be right to punish one man so as to set an
example to others. The answer to this is that the
wrongdoer is always an example to others when he is
brought into court, whether he is treated firmly or
leniently. If he is treated too leniently it is an illustration to others that the criminal law need not be
obeyed. The person who has broken the law has,
whether he is conscious of it or not, set an example
for others, and it is therefore not unjust to him if the
law seeks to prove that crime does not pay.

THE LAW OF TORTS

The fact that this branch of the law is entitled *tort*,
which is the French word for *wrong*, shows how
clearly it is connected with moral ideas, but here again
we must not exaggerate the relationship. In his
classic work, *The Common Law*, Mr. Justice Holmes
has said [25]:

> " Be the exceptions more or less numerous, the
> general purpose of the law of torts is to secure a
> man indemnity against certain forms of harm to
> person, reputation, or estate, at the hands of his

[25] p. 144.

neighbours, not because they are wrong, but because they are harms."

He concluded that the law of tort was a compromise between " the reasonable freedom of others with the protection of the individual from injury."

The idea of reasonable freedom involves, however, a moral concept, for it is not reasonable to act in an immoral way. Perhaps this has been stated in its most striking form by Lord Atkin in *Donoghue* v. *Stevenson* [26]: " the rule that you are to love your neighbour becomes in law, you must not injure your neighbour; and the lawyer's question: ' Who is my neighbour ? ' receives a restricted reply."

How restricted this reply is in the modern law is open to debate. There are those who think that in recent years the law of tort has been extended to a dangerous degree,[27] while there are others who believe that it is too restricted to meet in a satisfactory manner the changing conditions of the present day.[28] It would, of course, be possible to say that a man ought to pay for any injury caused by his act. Whether this was the conclusion reached in early English law has been strenuously debated, but the answer is still a doubtful one.[29] Perhaps the truth is that early law did not have a clear theory on this subject, just as the law today cannot be explained on a single principle. We find that the law as we know

[26] [1932] A.C. 562, 580.
[27] *Cf.* Mr. P. A. Landon, the editor of *Pollock on Torts*.
[28] *Cf.* Professor W. Friedmann: *Law and Social Change in Contemporary Britain*, 1951, pp. 73 *et seq.*
[29] Winfield discussed this question in his article " The Myth of Absolute Liability," (1926) 42 L.Q.R. 37.

it is almost equally divided between torts of strict
responsibility and those where liability arises only
if there is a particular mental element involved.   It
has been frequently said that the modern tendency is
to emphasise the doctrine of " no liability without
fault," but so great a common lawyer as Sir Frederick
Pollock suggested that this was an American rather
than an English interpretation.   He said [30]: " As an
English lawyer, I can only say that we never heard
of it here.   Stated as a general proposition, it is
contrary to the whole law of trespass, to much of the
law of nuisance, to the whole law of defamation and
to the responsibility of principals for their agents."
It is not true to say that these torts of strict liability
have no relation to the moral law because the tortfeasor is held liable even though he intended to do
no harm.   In these torts the law places the risk on
the actor, and not on the person who has been injured.
In all of them there is a conscious act done by the
actor, so that there is nothing arbitrary in the ascrip-
tion of responsibility to him.   If A enters on B's land
he has committed a trespass even though he has
reasonable grounds for believing that he himself is
the owner.   In certain cases this may bear hardly on
A, but the law cannot make an exception for hard
cases.   It is in the interest of general security that
anyone who intermeddles with the property of another
should be held responsible.

There is, however, another group of torts in which
the actor is held liable only if he has acted in an

[30] " A Plea for Historical Interpretation " (1923) 39 L.Q.R. 163,
167.

unreasonable manner. The most important of these
is the comparatively recent tort of negligence which
developed in the nineteenth century. But even here
the test of reasonableness is not a subjective one:
the standard required is that of the reasonable man.
It has been said [31] that the standard is that of the
man on the Clapham omnibus, but this is not strictly
accurate: it is the reasonable man on the Clapham
omnibus who supplies the measure. The courts, by
ascribing to him a reasonableness which the ordinary
man may not exercise as a general rule, can raise
the general sense of responsibility in the community.
Here again the law, instead of following slightly
behind public morality, as it is sometimes accused of
doing, can act as a moral leader.

There is a third type of tortious responsibility in
which the person is held responsible for the wrongful
act of another, even though he has in no way authorised it. The obvious illustration of this principle can
be found in the modern doctrine that a master is
liable for the wrongful acts of his servant, arising
out of and in the course of his employment, even
though the servant may be doing the act for his own
benefit and against the interest of his employer. This
principle, finally established in its full vigour by the
House of Lords in *Lloyd* v. *Grace, Smith & Co.*,[32]
has been criticised on the ground that it is unfair to
hold a master liable for a wrongful act which he has
done his best to guard against, but the answer is that
in placing the servant in a position in which he could

[31] *Hall* v. *Brooklands Racing Club* [1933] 1 K.B. p. 224.
[32] [1912] A.C. 716.

injure another he must be held to have assumed the
risk.[33]   As he will, as a general rule, benefit from
the servant's activity, it is morally right that he
should incur the loss if the servant commits a
wrongful act in these circumstances.

The same principle is applicable to what may be
called statutory negligence. Under the Factory Acts,
and other statutes of a similar nature, the owner of
a factory may be under an absolute duty to see that
the various safety regulations are carried out, and it is
no defence that this duty has been delegated to a
competent person who has failed to perform it. The
owner's absolute liability is in these circumstances
analogous to that of an insurer. He is held responsible, not because of his own fault, but because it is
felt that the risk should fall on him and not on the
employee. It is hardly surprising to find that those
who support the " strict liability " doctrine and
those who favour " no liability without fault " are
each able to base their arguments on moral grounds.
The truth is, that here we find, as happens so often in
the law, that there are two conflicting moral ideas,
and that the choice between them depends on what
is reasonable in the particular circumstances.

Perhaps no branch of English law has been so
frequently attacked on moral grounds as has the law
of torts, and it cannot be denied that there is some
basis for this criticism. One reason for this is that
the law has been constructed piecemeal with little
emphasis on general principles. We do not even know

[33] This is true even if the servant is the husband or wife of the
injured person: *Broom* v. *Morgan* [1953] 2 W.L.R. 737.

whether there is a law of tort or a law of torts. The law has even been reluctant to hold that all intentional " injuries " involve tortious liability. There are a considerable number of ways in which one person can intentionally injure another without subjecting himself to an action, but it would not be in the public interest to state them in detail. Three of them are, however, so obvious that I may cite them as illustrations. A man may insult another with impunity provided that, in doing so, he does not defame him or tend to cause a breach of the peace. Again, there is no law against the invasion of the privacy of another. And, finally, a man may make false statements of fact with impunity provided that he is not under a special duty of care, or that he does not bring himself within the narrow doctrine of legal fraud. It is not possible to bring these cases under a general principle that a man must not injure another without lawful excuse, because there is no such principle in English law. The second reason for the not infrequent conflicts between the law of torts and the moral law is that the judges have been reluctant to alter the law which has been made in the past, although the past no longer resembles the present. In no other branch of the law is it so true that the forms of action still rule us from their graves.[34]

Parts of the law of torts have been criticised as being morally inadequate, but it may be found that in some of these instances the civil law can get no clear guidance from the moral law. We can take as

[34] Maitland, *Forms of Action*, p. 296: " The forms of action we have buried, but they still rule us from their graves."

one example the problem concerning the duty of one person to help another in distress.[35]   This duty is clearly recognised at sea, but what would be the result of its application on land?   If I know that my poor neighbour is starving, is it my moral duty to share my food with him?   Until we are clear what the moral duty is in such cases it would be difficult for the law to attempt to deal with them.   Again, the law relating to invitees and licensees has been criticised on the ground that a host ought to take reasonable care to protect his guest from injury, but, on the other hand, it has been argued that a guest ought not to expect his host to assume such a burden.   Perhaps the most difficult problem relates to the so-called right to privacy: have I a moral right which will prevent my neighbours from discussing my private life?   If there is such a right where must its limits be drawn?   In these and other instances it is not the fault of the law that the present situation is unsatisfactory: it is due to uncertainty concerning the nature and extent of the moral responsibility involved.

CONTRACT

In discussing the basic principle of the law of contract Professor Corbin has said [36]:

" That portion of the field of law that is classified and described as the law of contracts attempts the realisation of reasonable expectations that have been induced by the making of a promise.   Doubtless,

[35] This is discussed at some length by Professor Ames in his article " Law and Morals," 22 Harvard L.R. 97, 112.
[36] *Law of Contracts*, 1950, vol. I, p. 2.   West & Co.

this is not the only purpose by which men have been motivated in creating the law of contracts; but it is believed to be the main underlying purpose, and it is believed that an understanding of many of the existing rules, and a determination of their effectiveness require a lively consciousness of this underlying purpose."

In other words, the moral basis of the law of contract is that the promisor has by his promise created a reasonable expectation that it will be kept: it is not based on the ground that he has agreed to be bound. A failure to realise this distinction has led to confusion in some cases dealing with mistake and with impossibility of performance.

Before I deal with the present law of contract I must say a few words concerning its history. The medieval law enforced covenants under seal and actions of debt, but the simple contract was not recognised in the common law courts. This did not mean that medieval man did not attach moral weight to a promise: on the contrary, as Professor Plucknett has said,[37] " The Church very early took a strong view on the sanctity of contractual relationships, insisting that in conscience the obligation of a contract was completely independent of writings, forms and ceremonies, and tried as far as she could to translate this moral theory into terms of law." The Church courts did not, however, succeed in establishing jurisdiction over contracts, so that the simple contract had

[37] *History of the Common Law*, p. 591.

to find another origin.[38] It did so in the " action of
case." As is known to all lawyers the first step began
with acts of misfeasance: a defendant had under-
taken to do something, but had done it so badly that
he had injured the plaintiff. The next advance was
when an action for nonfeasance was allowed, and
finally, in 1602, *Slade's Case*,[39] by recognising that
indebitatus assumpsit would lie, established the simple
contract as we know it. It is of importance to
remember that the law of contract found its origin in
the law of tort because this emphasises the fact that
contractual liability is based on the disappointment
of the promisee's reasonable expectations. The fact
that the promisor can establish that he did not intend
to make the agreement on which he is being sued is
therefore immaterial if he acted in such a manner as
to justify the promisee's belief in the promise.

It may be asked why it took the courts so long
before they recognised the simple contract. Perhaps
one reason is that in a more or less primitive community the idea of contract is of only slight
importance. It is not until commerce and industry
develop that promises begin to play a serious part in
the economic life of the country. Formal agreements
are made by a document under seal which proves
itself. A second reason for the late emergence of the
simple contract is found in the procedural difficulties
and in the methods of proof then available in the
courts.

[38] An excellent statement of the rather involved history of the
   English contract can be found in Cheshire and Fifoot, *The
   Law of Contract*, 3rd ed., 1953.
[39] 4 Rep. 92b.

After the simple contract had been established there was a danger that the field of liability might be extended to too great a degree. It was therefore necessary for the courts to limit it, and this they did by the development of the doctrine of consideration. It was not every promise which was binding in law, however much it might be binding in morals: it received legal validity only if the promisee had given some consideration for it. We thus get the bargain theory of contract super-imposed on the promise theory. It is based on the view that a person who has received a gratuitous promise ought not to be entitled to rely on it because, having given nothing for it, he ought not to expect anything in return.[40] Lord Mansfield, at the end of the eighteenth century, having had some training in the civil law, rejected this view, and attempted to reduce consideration merely to a form of evidence.[41] He was finally overruled by the House of Lords in *Rann* v. *Hughes* [42] in 1778, which left the law of contract as it is today. We can therefore say that the law recognises the obligation to perform a promise for which consideration has been given, but that it does not extend to moral obligations falling outside of this limit. A promise may, of course, act as an estoppel in certain circumstances against the assertion of a claim which the other party

[40] Lamont, *Principles of Moral Judgment*, p. 40, has said: " So strong indeed is this demand [for reciprocity] that in some legal systems there is a bias against the notion of enforceable unilateral obligations; a promise will not generally be binding unless it is balanced by some corresponding ' consideration.' "
[41] *Pillans* v. *Van Mierop* (1765) 3 Burr. 1663.
[42] (1778) 7 T.R. 350n.

has been led to believe has been waived,[43] but this does not affect the general principle concerning the necessity for consideration.

It is of interest to note that the Law Revision Committee, in its Sixth Interim Report, issued in 1937, suggested that the present law did not give sufficient weight to moral obligations in two regards. It recommended that a promise should be held legally binding, even in the absence of consideration, if there was sufficient evidence in writing, and if it was made with the intention that the promisee should act in reliance on it. It also recommended that a third-party beneficiary should be entitled to enforce a contract even though he himself had not given any consideration for the promise. As I was a member of the Law Revision Committee I may say that I am still of the opinion that these recommendations were sound, in spite of some learned criticism that has been advanced against them.[44]

It has been said that the English law is too strict in holding the promisor to his promise even when an obvious mistake on his part makes it morally unfair to hold him to it. X promises Y to sell him a painting for £10. X and Y both think that the painting is of little value. Thereafter it is established that the painting is a Rembrandt worth £20,000. Under English law the seller is bound by his promise. This is true, even if Y knew that the picture was a Rembrandt when he accepted X's promise. This

---

[43] *Central London Properties* v. *Hightrees House* [1947] K.B. 130.

[44] *Cf.* Cheshire and Fifoot, *Law of Contract*, 3rd ed., Part II, s. 6.

conclusion may seem to be unfair to X, but it is the legal expression of the moral law that a man must fulfil his promise, however hard this may be on him. There is much to be said for this English view, and it is not fanciful to suggest that the law has influenced the moral standards of the country in this regard. The phrase that " an Englishman's word is as good as his bond " is an illustration of the generally accepted principle that a man must perform his promise however disadvantageous this may be to him.

Closely analogous to this is the problem concerning impossibility of performance. In the seventeenth and eighteenth centuries the courts, in construing a contract, were inclined to do so in a strictly literal manner. If a man promised to do something, it was held that he must perform his promise or pay damages, however difficult or impossible the performance might prove to be. The classic case on this point is *Paradine* v. *Jane*,[45] in which the court said:

> " When the party by his own contract creates a duty or charge upon himself, he is bound to make it good, if he may, notwithstanding any accident by inevitable necessity, because he might have provided against it by his contract."

In recent years this strict method of construction has been ameliorated, the courts being more willing to read into the contract an implied term that the obligation to perform the contract is conditional upon its continued possibility. This was stated by Lord

[45] (1647) Aleyn 26.

Loreburn in *Tamplin S.S. Co.* v. *Anglo-Mexican Co.*[46]
in these words:

> " A court can and ought to examine the contract
> and the circumstances in which it was made, not,
> of course, to vary, but only to explain it, in order
> to see whether or not from the nature of it the
> parties must have made their bargain on the footing
> that a particular thing or state of things would
> continue to exist."

In the recent case of *British Movietonews* v. *London
Cinemas*[47] the House of Lords has made it clear that
this doctrine must not be carried too far. " An uncon-
templated turn of events " is not enough to enable a
court to substitute its notion of what is " just and
reasonable " for the contract as it stands: the test
is whether " a consideration of the terms of the
contract, in the light of the circumstances existing
when it was made, shows that they never agreed to
be bound in a fundamentally different situation which
has now unexpectedly emerged." A wholly abnormal
rise or fall in prices or a sudden depreciation of
currency will not, therefore, bring the contract to an
end. A convenient practical test is that of the
" officious bystander," envisaged by Lord Justice
MacKinnon in *Shirlaw* v. *Southern Foundries (1926)
Ltd.*,[48] who, at the moment when the contract is being
made, asks the parties whether they intended to be
bound if the circumstances, which are later said to

---

[46] [1916] 2 A.C. 397.
[47] [1952] A.C. 166, 185.
[48] *Shirlaw* v. *Southern Foundries (1926), Ltd.* [1939] 2 K.B.
206, 227.

frustrate the contract, should arise. If their answer would clearly be " No," then the court is entitled to hold that such an implied term is to be read into the contract. It follows from this that the courts in applying the doctrine of frustration are not attempting to alter the rule that a man is bound by his promise, even though it may seem hard, owing to a change in circumstances, to hold him to it: all that they will do is to interpret the original terms of the contract in a liberal manner.

The doctrine of frustration has, in the past, had the result of bringing the contract to an end when the frustrating event arose, so that the parties were left frozen in the positions they then held. This led to an unjust result when one of the parties had paid a sum in advance, without receiving anything in return. The Law Reform (Frustrated Contracts) Act, 1943, was therefore passed to deal with this point, but there are still one or two difficulties that remain.

Finally, when we are considering the relationship between the law of contract and the moral law, something must be said about the doctrine of public policy. I believe that it is important to distinguish between the two senses in which the phrase *public policy* is used, because a confusion between the two has led to a certain amount of misunderstanding. In the first sense *public policy* means that view of the public interest which may influence a court in establishing a precedent or in choosing one of two or more possible interpretations of a statute. It is obvious that in this sense public policy must be found in every branch of the law, for a judge will hesitate to establish a principle, which he must do whenever he has to decide a case of first impression, if he thinks that it is against the public interest. The fact that this influence may sometimes be an unconscious one, hides from us its great importance in the moulding of the law.[49]

Public policy is used, however, in a different sense in the law of contract. Here it means some reason on which a judge will base his refusal to enforce the ordinary contract rules. He holds, in these cases, that although there is an offer and acceptance and the necessary consideration, nevertheless the agreement is invalid on special grounds. It is obvious that in this second sense public policy must be approached with great hesitation because a power to depart from the ordinary law ought to be exercised only in exceptional circumstances. It is for this reason that public policy was described as an " unruly horse " in *Richardson* v. *Mellish*,[50] but this does not mean that a judge must enforce an agreement which is clearly against the public interest. No court in the world would enforce an agreement between two highwaymen to share the profits of their enterprise. Contracts which tend to immorality, contracts which are in conflict with the dignity of the court as in the case of wagers, and contracts which are against the economic interest of the country, have all been held to be against public policy. Here, the relationship between the law of contract and the moral law is directly

---

[49] On this point see Cardozo, *The Nature of the Judicial Process.*
[50] (1824) 2 Bing. 229, 242.

recognised by the courts, but they are careful to apply a moral law which is clear and certain. It is not enough that they themselves may disapprove of a particular course of conduct, for the law not infrequently enforces agreements which high-minded men may regard with disapprobation.

Although Sir George Jessel M.R.'s dictum [51] that " you are not lightly to interfere with this freedom of contract " is frequently quoted, Professor Stone [52] has pointed out that the English courts have taken a less doctrinaire position in this matter than did the U.S. Supreme Court in certain cases in the past. Liberty of contract, like other liberties, cannot be regarded as an absolute. In particular it must be subject to moral considerations, even though it may not always be easy to determine exactly what these are. Here, as in other parts of the law, the dividing line may be doubtful, but this will not prevent us from saying that certain cases clearly fall on one side or the other.

[51] *Printing and Numerical Registering Co.* v. *Sampson* (1875) L.R. 19 Eq. 462, 465.
[52] Julius Stone, *The Province and Function of Law*, 1950, pp. 256, 257.

THE OTHER BRANCHES OF THE
CIVIL LAW

4

THE OTHER BRANCHES OF THE CIVIL LAW

PROPERTY

THE right to private property has been explained on a number of different grounds. It has been based on (1) occupation, (2) work done in producing the property, (3) increment from property already owned, (4) inheritance, (5) gift, (6) exchange or barter, and (7) other forms of agreement. These grounds may vary in importance, depending on the particular circumstances under consideration. But, while accepting these practical explanations for the existence of private property, the natural law philosophers have based it on two more fundamental grounds. The first is the ground of reason, for reason teaches us that without private property the individual man would lose much of his individuality and his independence. A man without property must always be dependent on others, and he therefore lacks the capacity for freedom of action which is an essential part of the complete life. The second ground is that of natural instinct because even a young child can distinguish between those things which have been given to it or which it has in some way made its own, and those to which it has no claim. If this natural instinct is thwarted men may lose the incentive to work. This will be true especially if recognition is not given to the combination of this instinct with the instinct to protect one's family,

113

for the value of private property lies as much in the future as it does in the present.

On the other hand, it has often been pointed out that this so-called natural right to property is of little or no value unless it is protected by the law.[1] No one therefore has a moral claim to the legal protection of his property if it is being used against the social interest of the community. When we turn to the English law we find that the right in property has never been unqualified. The stock phrase that " an Englishman's home is his castle " is not true if it means that that castle is uncontrolled by the law. The phrase is nothing more than a particular expression of the general rule of law that the liberty of the individual is protected against unauthorised invasions by the servants of the Crown. It does not mean that there is a general principle that the Crown should not be given legal authority to enter private premises

---

[1] N. Micklem, *Law and the Laws*, 1952. Sweet & Maxwell, Ltd. At p. 83 the author says: "It is claimed that man has a natural right to private property and to testamentary disposition of it. Property corresponds with ownership and possession, but these latter are conditions constituted and defined by law. Property cannot well be defined except in terms of rights created and recognised by law, and it is not profitable to lay down the formal principle that we have natural rights to such legal rights as the contemporary juridical system may afford us."

On the other hand, James Lorimer in *The Institutes of Law—A Treatise of the Principles of Jurisprudence as Determined by Nature* (2nd ed., 1880), states categorically that (p. 229): "The right to reproduce and multiply our being involves the right of transmitting to our offspring the conditions of the existence which we confer." It is some comfort, although not of any practical value, to realise that our present Death Duties are against the laws of nature and must meet with her disapproval.

where this is deemed to be necessary in the public interest. Nor does English law recognise any principle which will enable a person to use his property without any regard for the interests of his neighbours. The whole law of public and private nuisance is a denial of such an unreasonable and anti-social doctrine. Moreover, under the doctrine of *Rylands* v. *Fletcher*,[2] an occupier of land, who creates an unreasonable risk on it, will be held strictly liable for any injury resulting from the dangerous situation. It is therefore incorrect to say that the English law of property is absolute in nature, and that it fails to recognise the moral obligations of the owner.

Under the law of property we must consider the law relating to inheritance, for it has been correctly said that inheritability is an important element in the concept of private property. Whether it is also an essential element is more open to doubt. Strange to say it has never been made clear whether this so-called natural right of inheritance is one attached to the owner of the property or is regarded as being vested in his heirs. English law has only recently recognised, and then only to a strictly limited degree, the rights of the members of the family. It has allowed a husband and father to disinherit completely by his will his wife and children who, during his lifetime, were legally entitled to his support. This rule, which has given rise to many cases which could not be morally justified, has been tempered by the Inheritance (Family Provision) Act, 1938,[3] but it is still true to

---

[2] (1868) L.R. 3 H.L. 330.
[3] Some persons believe that this Act is too narrow in its scope.

say that in English law there is a far greater power of disinheritance than in almost all other legal systems.

English law has been criticised on the ground that it gives greater protection to property than it does to human rights, but this criticism, which is not without some justification,[4] especially in the administration of the criminal law, may be exaggerated if we forget the political and social role which property has played in English history. When John Locke [5] wrote of the fundamental rights to " life, liberty, and property," this association of liberty was a natural one for an Englishman to make for, as Professor McIlwain has said, English liberty was based on the control of the purse strings.[6] It was in the basic constitutional principle that no tax could be levied without the consent of Parliament that modern democracy found its origin.

---

[4] On the other hand, Professor Roscoe Pound in *Social Control Through Law*, 1942, says at p. 60: " If, therefore, the law secures property and contract more elaborately and more adequately than it secures personality, it is not because the law rates the latter less highly than the former, but because legal machinery is intrinsically well adapted to securing the one and intrinsically ill adapted to securing the other."

[5] *Second Treatise of Civil Government*, 1690.

[6] In *Political Thought in the West* (1932) McIlwain says (p. 394): " If I were asked which of the famous maxims into which the political thought of the world has at times been compressed is the one which on the whole least comprises the living political conceptions of the later middle ages, my choice, I imagine, would be rather unexpected, and not in all cases accepted, but it is one which my study of this period makes me willing to defend. It is the aphorism from Seneca's *De Beneficiis*, ' Ad reges enim potestas omnium pertinet: ad singulos, proprietas '—to kings belongs authority over all: to private persons property." Professor Plucknett in his *History of the Common Law*, 4th ed., p. 37, agrees with this view.

From the social standpoint the law of property has been equally important, for it bound the family together from one generation to another, and emphasised the importance of family traditions. It is not surprising that Edmund Burke should have taken as his analogy the strict settlement when he said [7]: " One of the first and most leading principles on which the commonwealth and the laws are consecrated, is lest the temporary possessors and life-renters in it, unmindful of what they have received from their ancestors, or of what is due to their posterity, should act as if they were the entire masters." Perhaps in no other country in the world is this sense of partnership between the past, the present, and the future, so strong as it is in England, and this is due in no small degree to the mode of thought established by the law of property. This feeling of duty to the past and to the future is a moral one, so that it is true to say that even in the law of property, which is sometimes regarded as cold and lifeless, there is a close relationship between legal and moral ideas.

COMMERCIAL LAW

It is not surprising to find that commercial law and moral law are closely related, because both commerce and industry depend on good faith. It is difficult to envisage an economic system which does not assume as a basic premise that men can rely on each other's promises. These promises may be given additional force by the law, but even in the absence of law they

[7] 5 *Collected Works* (1808) at 181.

must be recognised as obligatory by the commercial community if it is to exist at all.[8] It is noteworthy that the Law Merchant was not created by the State, but was taken over by the courts long after it had been firmly established.

There are two other reasons why the moral element figures so largely in commercial law. The first is that, as it is largely international both in origin and in character, it may be said to be a type of *jus gentium*— a body of obligatory rules based on a general conviction of what is right and wrong. If men did not recognise these common moral principles it would be difficult for them to agree on a common law. The second reason is that the canon law exerted a strong influence on the Law Merchant during its formative period. Professor Plucknett has said [9]: " The Church, too, was exerting a growing influence upon mercantile practice. Particularly in the law of contract the Church asserted the principle of keeping faith—a principle which must lie at the root of commercial life."

This good faith is the basis of the law of principal and agent. The principal must protect his agent, and the agent must not take any advantage of his principal. Thus if, in the course of his agency, he receives information which is of value, he must use this for the benefit of his principal and not for his own advantage. The same principle is found in the law of partnership, for each partner must be able to

[8] Professor Max Weber has made the influence of these extra-legal systems the main thesis of his sociological contributions to legal philosophy.
[9] *History of the Common Law*, p. 621.

rely on the complete good faith of the other. Again, in the law of insurance, an insured person must make full disclosure of all relevant facts even if he has not been asked for them specifically.

It may be asked, however: How can the law merchant claim to be consonant with the moral law as long as it contains the maxim *caveat emptor*? The answer is, that this maxim, which Professor Radin [10] has described as " bad Latin and, from the Roman point of view, worse law," is not part of the law merchant, but a survival from the early common law. We can see how the merchants have attempted to narrow its scope, in so far as it is applicable to them, if we study the Sale of Goods Act, 1893. The implied conditions and warranties which are binding on the seller are nothing more than a legal expression of the high standards recognised by respectable merchants. It is unfortunate that when we turn to the sale or lease of real property we find that the standard is so low that no decent man would accept it as a guide. It is an astonishing fact that a man may sell a field which to his knowledge has been sprayed with a poison deadly to animals,[11] or lease a house which contains a boiler likely to explode without giving any adequate warning.[12] This is one instance where there is an

---

[10] *The Lawful Pursuit of Gain*, 1931, p. 54.
[11] *Sutton* v. *Temple* (1843) 12 M. & W. 52.
[12] *Bottomley* v. *Bannister* [1932] 1 K.B. 458. In *Robbins* v. *Jones* (1863) 15 C.B.(N.S.) p. 240, Erle C.J., in a judgment written by Willes J. said: " Fraud apart, there is no law against letting a tumble-down house." This is self-evident, but it does not follow from this that the vendor ought not to be under a duty to disclose a concealed danger to a purchaser who has no reason to know that it exists.

obvious gap between the English law and the moral law as recognised by almost everyone who is not a lawyer.

English commercial law is probably less strict than the moral law in regard to untruthful statements carelessly made. A man who is not deliberately fraudulent, so as to bring himself within the technical rules of the tort of deceit, can take liberties with the truth which under the moral law he owes to his neighbour. In company law an increasingly strict duty of care has been placed on those who issue accounts and prospectuses, but in other branches of the law carelessness may still prove to be profitable to the man who has not got too strict a conscience.

Perhaps the most difficult problem in commercial law concerns what has been termed unfair competition. To what extent may one competitor attempt to get the better of another? [13] Here we may find that there are practices which cannot be justified on moral grounds, but which for practical reasons the law cannot reach. It is probable, however, that this field may be developed in the future, in particular in relation to misleading advertisements.

---

[13] This question is closely related to the tort and crime of conspiracy. To what extent, and for what purposes, may men combine together to injure another? The answer given by the House of Lords in *Crofter Hand Woven Harris Tweed Co.* v. *Veitch* [1942] A.C. 435 is that disinterested malevolence will give rise to legal liability, but that a conspiracy, carried on by lawful means, is not illegal if its purpose is to advance the interests of the participants. Professor Friedmann has discussed this problem in his valuable book *Legal Theory*, pp. 348 *et seq.*

COMPANY LAW

It has been said that a corporation has " neither a soul to be damned nor a body to be kicked." It is this fact which has given rise to a number of moral problems. The law has created these artificial persons, who own nearly two-thirds of the property in this country, but although immensely wealthy and powerful, they are themselves completely helpless. An artificial person, being a mere conception or idea, can do no acts of any kind: it cannot even appoint an agent to act in its name. The law therefore arranges for the appointment of these agents, and provides rules which determine what acts of theirs will bind the corporation. It is obvious that this extraordinary system by which a lifeless and artificial person is held responsible for the acts of living men must give rise to difficult moral questions. These are best exemplified in the case of the business company.

The major purpose of a business company is to allow individuals to engage in a commercial activity without being subjected to unlimited liability. The only liability which the shareholders incur is the payment to the company of the price of their shares. The person who trades with the company is expected to know that he has no claim whatsoever against the incorporators or the shareholders. The situation is aggravated by the fact that the incorporator of a company may sell to the artificial person he has created a factory or other property, and in return for this he receives a security which enables him to recover the property he has sold to the company if the company goes into liquidation.[14]   The courts have, therefore, in some cases sought to pierce the corporate veil in an attempt to place increased personal liability on the human beings in control of these artificial persons, but these attempts have not proved successful.   The moral question which arises in these cases concerns the ability of those in control of the company to engage in transactions which, at no risk to themselves, may prove profitable for them, but, if unsuccessful, must be paid for by third persons who, in many instances, are unable to understand the intricacies of company law.[15]   The law has attempted to limit the risk by increasing the safeguards against fraudulent practices, but it is obvious that it cannot always protect the creditors of these artificial persons. This, however, is inevitable because the doctrine of limited liability would lose its value if in every hard case the corporate veil could be pierced.   Here the law consciously realises that it may on occasion give rise to situations which cannot be justified on moral grounds, but it does so on the ground that this is a small price to pay for the great benefit which has

14 *Salomon* v. *Salomon & Co., Ltd.* [1897] A.C. 22.
15 This is true, in particular, in regard to the doctrine of *ultra vires* which may enable a company to repudiate liability on the ground that its officers, including the directors, have engaged in the company's name in activities which lay outside its purposes as stated in the Memorandum of Association.   The Committee on Company Law Amendment (popularly known as the Cohen Committee after its chairman Lord Cohen) recommended in its report, 1945, that this doctrine should be abolished but this recommendation was not incorporated in the Companies Act, 1948.

accrued to the community by the creation of these artificial persons.

The second problem, which is more difficult from the theoretical than from the practical standpoint, concerns the tortious and criminal liability of these artificial persons. It is said that, as the law of tort and the law of crime are concerned with the wrongful acts committed by the tortfeasor and by the criminal, it follows that an artificial person which has been created by the State cannot commit such acts. This is obviously true, but it does not follow from this that a corporation cannot be held responsible for the wrongful acts of its servants. It has taken many years, however, for the law to realise that there is nothing wrong in principle in holding a corporation liable under such circumstances. A corporation obviously cannot commit an assault, but one of its servants can, and it is therefore for the servant's act that the corporation is held responsible. There is no real moral problem here because, as the artificial person lives and benefits by the acts of its servants, so it must be held responsible for their faults.

A third question of great difficulty concerns the relation between the directors and officers of a business company on the one hand, and the shareholders of the company on the other. Technically, the directors and the officers, although they may be chosen by the shareholders, are neither trustees nor agents for them. The legal duty of the officials is to the company and not to those who own its shares. As a result, a director commits no breach of trust or breach of agency if he takes advantage of any inside information which he may have obtained either to buy or to sell shares. The Company Law Amendment Committee reached the conclusion that such acts were obviously in conflict with business morality, but on the other hand, it felt that it would be difficult to enact provisions which would prohibit such unfair practices on the part of directors. It therefore recommended that directors should be forced to state publicly the transactions which they themselves carried out in the shares of the company. It was felt that the force of public opinion would be sufficient to prohibit such practices. This recommendation has been incorporated in the Companies Act, 1948.[16] This is an interesting illustration of recognition by the law that outside sanctions may in fact be more effective than the purely legal ones.

EQUITY

It is obvious from its name that equity is closely related to the moral law.[17] When its history begins towards the end of the fourteenth century the common law has become more or less rigid as the judges regard themselves as strictly bound by the established rules.[18] Little relief against hard cases can be found in legislation because this works only intermittently. Fortunately there is a reserve of justice in the King so that those who cannot get relief elsewhere present

[16] s. 195.
[17] The nature and history of English equity are fully covered by Sir Carleton Allen, *Law in the Making*, 5th ed., 1951, Chap. V.
[18] Maitland, *Equity*, 1910, p. 5: "But in the fourteenth century the courts of law have become very conservative and are given to quashing writs which differ in material points from those already in use."

their petitions to him, praying for some remedy. He cannot alter the established law, but he can prevent its being used in an unjust manner. Perhaps we can find a modern analogy to this in our present law establishing the death penalty for murder. The law says that the penalty for murder shall be death, but the Queen, through the Home Secretary, may reprieve the convicted murderer. Similarly, the King, through the Lord Chancellor, did not deny that the trustee (to use the modern term) was the legal owner of the trust property, but he forced him to carry out his moral duty to the beneficiary of the trust. In time third persons, who knew or ought to have known of the trust, also became bound by it. The trust developed because there was no way in which the common law could deal with this situation, for, as Maitland has said,[19] " we have to remember that in the fourteenth century—and that, in the present context, is the important century—the common law had not yet begun to enforce ' the simple contract '— it had not yet evolved the action of assumpsit out of the action of trespass."

It is no exaggeration to say that the invention of the trust was the greatest invention ever made by English lawyers. It has created a concept which has proved of extraordinary practical value by giving to the English law a flexibility which is lacking in those systems which are based on the Roman law. But it has been of equally great importance from the moral standpoint. It has emphasised that whenever a

[19] *Equity*, p. 28.

relationship of trust has been created between two persons, then a high standard of moral duty must be applied to it. This standard is not that which is necessarily held by the average man, but is one which the courts have felt that a man of probity would instinctively accept.[20]

In summing up the contributions made by equity Maitland has said [21]: " In my view equity has added to our legal system, together with a number of detached doctrines, one novel and fertile institution, namely, the trust; and three novel and fertile remedies, namely, the decree for specific performance; the injunction, and the judicial administration of estates." These three remedies have one thing in common—they act *in personam*. A man is ordered to do something, and if he fails to act then the Lord Chancellor can bring force to bear on him. It is not necessary for me to point out here that the exercise of these remedies has in time become fixed within determinate lines so that, by the beginning of the nineteenth century, equity had acquired the same firmness (or rigidity, to use a less flattering term) which marked the common law. The fluidity of the original equity was no longer needed because a remedy against the injustice of an outmoded law could now be sought in Parliament. The reforms of the past one hundred and fifty years show how effective this has been.

[20] I have discussed the significance of the trust concept in the field of government in my Cardozo lecture *English Contributions to the Philosophy of Law*, 1949, Oxford University Press, pp. 23 *et seq.*
[21] *Equity*, p. 22.

It has long been a disputed question whether the morality which the Lord Chancellor exercised was a personal one or one which he took from the canon law. As the Lord Chancellor was, until the end of the sixteenth century, a distinguished cleric, it is inevitable that the canon law, in which he was trained, must have played an important role.[22] It is equally true that the whole tradition of English life and thought must have influenced him not to place too much emphasis on general principles, but to seek to answer each problem as it was presented to him on grounds of practical common sense. The reasonable man of the English law is never far away, not even from the Courts of Chancery.

QUASI-CONTRACT

The branch of the law which was formerly called quasi-contract has recently tended to change its name to Unjust Enrichment.[23] Such a change is not surprising because this part of the law has only a comparatively recent history. Its new name is useful because it emphasises the moral origin of the various rules comprised under this heading. It is based on the principle that a man who has acquired a benefit

---

[22] But Maitland said, *Equity*, p. 14: "Blackstone, I think, greatly overrates the influence of Roman and canon law in the history of equity."

[23] The judgments of Lord Wright have had an important influence on the development of this branch of the law in England. So have the academic contributions made by Sir Percy Winfield. In no other branch of the English law is the influence of American legal thought more marked because much of the most constructive work has been done in the United States. Professor Keener of the Columbia University Law School was a pioneer in this field.

at the expense of another ought not to retain it. Thus, if A without permission uses B's motor-car to earn hire, it is morally just that B should recover this from A. Again, if A is forced to pay B's debt to C he ought to be entitled to recover this sum from B. It is obvious that unjust enrichment will take many forms, with the result that the law has dealt with this principle under many different headings, the best known of which is that of money had and received to the use of another. Because it has been divided in this way, we sometimes tend to forget how important this principle is in practice.[24]

When the principle of unjust enrichment was developing in the eighteenth century, English law was still governed by the forms of action. It was necessary, therefore, to find a form of action under which this type of claim could be fitted, and the only possible one was *indebitatus assumpsit*. This necessitated the allegation of an implied contract, even though it was obvious that the contract was in truth fictitious. Now that the forms of an action have been abolished, it is reasonable to suggest that the fiction should be disregarded, and that the true nature of unjust enrichment be given legal recognition. This course has not, however, been adopted by the courts.[25] They have taken the view that because the precedent cases of a century ago referred to a fictitious contract, therefore they must find a fictitious contract today,

---

[24] In *The Province of the Law of Tort*, 1931, pp. 155 *et seq.*, Professor Winfield gave a list of eleven "pure quasi-contracts" ranging all the way from salvage to unauthorised gains of an agent.

[25] *Sinclair* v. *Brougham* [1914] A.C. 398.

even though the reason for this fiction no longer exists. Fortunately, it is possible to find an implied contract in almost any situation, however absurd this implication may be, so that the problem, although of great theoretical interest, is only of minor practical importance. Perhaps an illustration may show how this rule works in practice. In *Reading* v. *The King*,[26] the plaintiff Reading, a sergeant in the British Army, was during the war stationed in Cairo. At that time a highly lucrative trade in smuggling dope was carried on in that city. Reading was given large sums to sit next to the driver of a lorry so that his uniform would give the impression that the lorry was an official one. When this traffic was discovered, the Crown seized the £30,000 which Reading had deposited in a bank. He claimed the return of this money, but the Crown defended on the ground that it was money had and received to its use. The House of Lords, affirming the Court of Appeal which had affirmed the trial judge, held that, as the plaintiff was in the service of the Crown, there was an implied contract that any profit which he had made by the use of the Crown's property would belong to the Crown. It is an interesting question what the position would have been if a man, not a soldier, had stolen the uniform, and had then used it as Reading did in this case. It would be difficult to argue that the thief in stealing the uniform had entered into an implied contract with the Crown, but, on the other hand, it is impossible to believe that he would be entitled to keep the money which he had acquired by the use of the Crown's

26 [1951] A.C. 507.

property. It may be suggested that it is unfortunate that the fiction concerning the implied contract has remained in the law, because it suggests that this type of claim has to be bolstered up by an obviously unrealistic allegation, when, in fact, the true moral basis on which the claim is based is clear and uncontroversial.

A minor point in this branch of the law is of interest from the moral standpoint. To what extent ought a person who has voluntarily conferred a benefit on another thereafter ask for repayment? The English law has tended to take the view that virtue ought to be its own reward, and that, therefore, the volunteer cannot ask for repayment. If X finds Y's motor-car abandoned on the road and does necessary repairs to it while Y is absent seeking help, he cannot ask to be repaid for his trouble. The Roman law and the modern Continental law give greater rights to the volunteer, but it is not clear whether that solution is more satisfactory than is the stricter view of the common law.[27]

FAMILY LAW

English law, as must the law of any civilised nation, recognises the moral importance of marriage to the community. It therefore provides that a marriage cannot be entered into without the necessary forms,

---

[27] In Buckland and McNair's *Roman Law and Common Law*, 1936, Cambridge University Press, after stating (p. 258) that, " *Negotiorum gestio* is an institution which is not recognised in our law with the generality it had under Justinian " the two learned authors make a detailed comparison of the two principles.

and the forms which it requires make it certain that a marriage cannot be celebrated because of a momentary whim. The law shows its favour to marriage by providing that any contract, provision in a will, or other act which can be regarded as an unreasonable restraint on marriage is against public policy. Similarly, any provision which may tend to interfere with the continuance of a marriage is invalid. Anyone who entices a husband or wife does so at his or her legal peril. In the past, the law has encouraged marriage by imposing certain disadvantages on those who live together without benefit of clergy, especially in regard to illegitimate children. Today there is one striking exception to this general principle of benevolence to marriage in the Income Tax Law, because it favours those who live in sin. Under this law the incomes of a husband and wife are regarded as one, but this does not apply to those persons who are prepared to accept a less formal arrangement.

Perhaps the most radical change in recent years in the moral and legal conception of family life can be found in the altered position of the wife, both in regard to her husband and to their children. It is impossible today to read such a case as *Re Agar-Ellis* [28] without a feeling of shock. The husband had, before the marriage, promised his wife that any children they might have would be brought up as Roman Catholics. He later changed his mind, and when the mother tried to influence the three children he removed them from her care and allowed her to visit them only once a month. The eldest daughter,

[28] (1883) 24 Ch.D. 317.

aged seventeen, asked for permission to spend a few weeks with her mother during the summer vacation. The Court of Appeal, although clearly of the opinion that the father was acting in an unfair manner in refusing this permission, held that it must " leave to him the responsibility of exercising that power which nature has given him by the birth of the child." Apparently nature takes the view that the birth of the child gives less power to the mother in spite of the more arduous part she plays in this matter.   Lord Justice Bowen said [29] : " To neglect the natural jurisdiction of the father over the child until the age of twenty-one would be really to set aside the whole course and order of nature, and it seems to me it would disturb the very foundation of family life."   In recent years the Court of Appeal has held that a marriage is a partnership, and that husbands and wives have equal rights and duties. [30]   It does not seem that " the foundation of family life " has been unduly disturbed by this later decision.

The law has adopted a new attitude in regard to illegitimate children.   In the past it was thought right that the sins of their fathers should be visited on these children, because it was felt that their miserable condition would be a warning against the results of immorality.   Today the law is more charitable to those who are unfortunate.

When we turn to the subject of divorce we find that the law on this subject tends to be of a fluctuating nature because there is no general agreement

---

[29] At p. 336.
[30] *Rimmer* v. *Rimmer* [1953] 1 Q.B. 63.

concerning the moral law. There are those who, primarily on religious grounds, regard the whole conception of divorce as immoral, holding that a marriage is indissoluble. There are others who regard it as immoral to continue the marriage-tie after both or even one of the parties desires its dissolution. The English law is a compromise between these two views, and it will continue to be a battle-ground until there is a general agreement on the moral questions involved. The Royal Commission which is now considering this question has an unenviable task.

The English law does not recognise the family as a legal institution. It therefore has not got anything resembling the French *conseil de famille*. Under the English law the adult who is mentally feeble but not insane, can waste his substance without any control by members of the family. It has been suggested that the negative English attitude on this point is an unmoral one, but the answer probably is that it would be extremely difficult in practice to establish a satisfactory rule. Moreover, the system of marriage settlements, which is common in this country, makes the problem a less important one than it is in other countries.

Practice and Procedure

The law relating to practice and procedure would at first sight seem to have no relationship to morals. We tend to think of it as a body of technical rules which for some reason is a necessary evil in the administration of justice. There is a feeling that if we could only avoid these rules we should be more able to attain natural justice. This is one reason why administrative tribunals are often welcomed with such enthusiasm, but experience has shown that unless they are governed by definite rules of procedure they tend to become arbitrary.

In early law procedure was primarily religious, being based on the ordeal, the trial by battle, or the wager of law. The ordeal and the trial by battle were both attempts to obtain a Divine decision in matters that were thought to be too difficult for human judgment. The wager of law was based on the idea that a man would not swear to the truth of something which he knew was false.

With the abolition of the trial by ordeal in 1215 it became necessary to find some other method by which the truth could be determined, so trial by jury was gradually evolved. For many centuries it has supplied an efficient method of justice which has been adopted throughout the Anglo-Saxon world. Today in England it has been displaced in most civil cases, but it still remains, and undoubtedly will continue to remain, in those civil cases in which the reputation of one of the parties is at stake, and in all serious criminal trials.

At first sight it seems difficult to justify the jury system on theoretical grounds. It does not seem logical to provide that a case should be tried by a judge of great experience and argued by highly trained counsel, but that the final decision should be left to twelve ordinary men and women. This is, of course, true, but the historical justification for the jury is found in the protection it gave against executive and judicial tyranny. Even the Act of Settlement, 1701, was no protection in the prosecutions for treason, sedition and libel brought at the end of the eighteenth century because the judges shared in the political ideas of the government. It was the courage and independence shown by the juries which protected liberty at that time.

There is a second justification for the jury system which is more important today than the historical one. It is found in the realisation that in determining questions of fact even the fairest of men may unconsciously be affected by their prejudices so that there is always a risk in leaving the decision to a single man. The strength of the jury is found in the fact that in the jury room the various prejudices which may to some extent influence the different jurors tend to cancel each other out in the course of their deliberations. This, of course, is not always true, especially when there is general prejudice against an individual or a group, but nevertheless the jury has always been regarded as a symbol of fairness and impartiality. It has given to the people at large confidence in the administration of justice, and it has therefore given to the law that moral support which I believe is essential in any efficient legal system.

But the jury system has played an equally important moral role in an indirect manner. It has acted as a great school in the morality of government, for it has taught the ordinary man that he must take his part in the administration of justice. It has not always been an easy part to play, for until *Bushel's Case* [31] in 1670 finally established their independence, jurymen were not infrequently punished if their verdicts did not satisfy those in authority, but the juries by their courage succeeded in overthrowing this doctrine. There is no part of English history which is a better tribute to the English character than is that connected with the jury.

Jury service has also taught the ordinary man that he must listen to both sides in any dispute. The law, as I have said, is a great teacher, and nowhere are its lessons more effective than in the jury box. It is a difficult thing to be fair, but a man who has listened to a trial which is properly conducted will have had an illustration of fairness in action which he may never forget.

The jury has had another indirect effect on English thought. As has been frequently pointed out, it is due to the existence of the jury that hearsay evidence is so carefully excluded at a trial, for it is rightly felt that such evidence may be given more weight than it properly deserves. But in time legal thinking tends to influence lay thinking, and I believe that the average Englishman's dislike and distrust of rumour and scandal in political and social life is due in part to the fact that he has been taught that hearsay evidence is not to be believed.

It is not surprising that procedure should be related to the moral law for its primary purpose is to enable

---

[31] Vaughan 135. Bushel had been one of the jury which acquitted William Penn of unlawful assembly, and in consequence he had been committed to prison.

those who have to decide a dispute to reach a just conclusion. In so far as it departs from this purpose it conflicts with morality. It cannot be denied, however, that legal history shows that procedure tends to develop almost a life of its own, and that sooner or later it becomes necessary to reform the rules which have become a hindrance rather than a help. But this tendency is not found in the law alone, for in almost every human activity form may gradually encroach upon substance. This is true even in religion, and no one who has had anything to do with the army or navy or any other governmental department can fail to realise this. The fact that legal procedure has deviated from time to time from its original purpose must therefore not blind us to the fact that it has made important contributions to the moral thought of this country. In his valuable book *The Quest of Justice* [32] the late Professor Harold Potter said [33]:

" The fight for human justice must be on a procedural plane, since procedure may determine how far the truth can come out. . . . It is after all a procedural rule that a man must be heard on his own behalf. . . . To say of the rule that it is required by ' natural justice ' does not alter the fact that it is essentially procedural and that it represents a difference from rules sometimes elsewhere observed. . . . Justice can be done without procedural rules, but this may be in spite of their absence as well as because of it. An analysis of the

[32] 1952.
[33] pp. 28, 29.

infamous trial and subsequent execution of Sir Walter Raleigh may bring this home."

This is an eloquent warning that those who are ready to scrap rules of procedure for what they regard as " natural justice " may be sacrificing true justice for the sake of temporary convenience.

EVIDENCE

One would not expect to find that the law relating to evidence gives rise to many moral problems, but there are in fact a number which are of considerable interest.

The first one concerns the oath which all witnesses are required to take unless they refuse to do so on grounds of conscience, in which case they are allowed to affirm.   The solemn oath is one of the most ancient parts of legal procedure, and is found in almost all legal systems.   The ancient method of trial, if it can be called that, by wager of law is an illustration of the great weight attached to the oath in medieval times, for the party who was given the right to wage his law was able to win his case if he could get the requisite number of eleven compurgators to swear that they believed that he was in the right.   To what extent the oath has persuaded witnesses to tell the truth is a disputed question.   It can be argued with force that a man who is prepared to lie when he has not taken an oath is hardly the type who will be much influenced by the additional threat of a Divine sanction.   The nonchalance with which people are prepared to swear to an affidavit which they have never read is some evidence that the oath today is little more than an empty gesture in most instances. It may even be said that the oath tends to bring religion into disrepute as it is regarded as a mere formality by many persons. Against these arguments we must balance the views of many experienced judges who believe that the oath does tend to influence witnesses, and that it reduces the amount of perjury.

Closely connected with the oath was the rule, which strange to say existed until 1850, that no party to a civil action nor any person who was interested in the result, could give evidence. This rule was based in part on the theory that a party or other interested person would be tempted to give perjured evidence, and that if he were allowed to do so after taking the oath he would be endangering his immortal soul. To prevent this he was prohibited from giving evidence. Strange to say the rule was not applied in equitable proceedings for in them the affidavits of the parties were always admissible.

Perhaps the most direct influence of morality on the admission of evidence is found in the rule which provides that in most criminal cases neither a husband nor a wife is a compellable witness against the other, and that even if he or she is prepared to give such evidence it will not be admitted without the consent of the other spouse. Various grounds can be given for this rule, but the obvious one is that it shocks one's sense of moral fitness that a husband or wife should be allowed to give evidence against the other. The fact that in some totalitarian trials wives have been called to denounce their husbands, is abhorrent to most people.

It has been argued that on moral grounds a similar rule ought to apply in the case of parents and children, but the law has refused to take this further step on practical grounds. In practice such evidence is rarely called because it would be almost impossible to force a recalcitrant parent to give evidence against his or her child.

It is for a similar reason that there seems to be no case in which a clergyman has been called to give evidence concerning any confession made to him. From the strictly legal standpoint the clergyman can probably not refuse to testify, but it is almost inconceivable that any judge would attempt to force him to do so. On the other hand, the rule that no legal adviser is permitted, without his client's consent, to disclose any communication made to him by his client, is not based on moral grounds, but is a necessary part of the proper administration of justice. A difficult question arises in connection with the medical profession, because the law and medicine are not in agreement concerning the degree of immunity which should be granted to doctors. Here again common sense has proved useful in keeping the issue a theoretical rather than a practical one.

CONFLICT OF LAWS

In the field of conflict of laws questions of morality have given rise to some difficult problems although there are only a limited number of cases on this subject. Ought an English court enforce a foreign contract, which is valid by the law of the country in which it was made, if the English court deems the contract to be in contravention of some essential principle of justice or morality? The leading case on this point is *Kaufman* v. *Gerson*,[34] in which the defendant had been coerced by the plaintiff into signing a contract in France by threats of a criminal prosecution against her husband. Such a contract is regarded as valid under French law as it is thought to be in the interest of all the parties that repayment of money misappropriated should be made either by the wrongdoer himself or by his family rather than that a criminal prosecution should be brought. The Court of Appeal held, however, that no cause of action could be grounded on such a contract in the courts of this country, even though made by domiciled French parties in France, because " to enforce a contract so procured would be to contravene what by the law of this country is deemed an essential moral interest." This decision gave great offence to French lawyers as they denied that the French law on this point, which is followed by many other countries, is immoral, but, apart from the particular facts of the case, the general principle is obviously correct. It is clear that Mrs. Warren, in *Mrs. Warren's Profession*,[35] could not have sued her partner, Sir George Crofts, in an English court for an accounting of the profits arising from the business activities which they pursued in Belgium although those activities were legally recognised there. The question concerning the morality of a legal provision may be a fine one. Thus in *Re Macartney* [36]

[34] [1904] 1 K.B. 591.
[35] George Bernard Shaw's play written in 1894.
[36] [1921] 1 Ch. 522.

Astbury J. held that " the general recognition of the permanent rights of illegitimate children and their spinster mothers as recognised in Malta is contrary to the established policy of this country," but this view, which has been severely criticised, would almost certainly not be accepted today. English law and English morality have travelled a long way in this matter since 1921.

The question of morality has been of particular importance in recent years in those cases in which the validity of a foreign decree confiscating the property of an oppressed minority has been at issue, and also in those cases where obvious duress was exercised to force a person to surrender his assets. The courts have held that discriminatory legislation would not be recognised in relation to property, held in this country, on the ground that such legislation was in conflict with morality, but some doubt may have been cast on this principle in *Kahler* v. *Midland Bank, Ltd.*[37]

Perhaps the most disputed questions in the conflict of laws have arisen in regard to polygamy. At one time it was thought that the English courts would refuse to recognise polygamy in any way, but it has now been held that a polygamous marriage, if validly contracted abroad, must be recognised as a valid

---

[37] [1950] A.C. 24. Concerning this case Professor Cheshire has said (*Private International Law*, 4th ed., 1952) at p. 140: " This decision has been the subject of damaging criticism. It certainly seems an unfortunate application of the rules of private international law that the undisputed owner of property in London, who, as the price of permission to leave Czecho-Slovakia, had been compelled to sign a document placing that property at the virtual disposal of a Prague bank under German control, should in effect be divested of his ownership."

marriage in this country. (*Baindail* v. *Baindail* [38] and *Srini Vasan* v. *Srini Vasan*.[39]) This is only common sense because the Christian doctrine that a marriage must be to one woman only does not apply in many non-Christian countries. It does not follow from this that a man who is domiciled in England, and whose personal law therefore is English, is entitled to enter into a polygamous marriage in a foreign country which recognises such marriages. The question whether a marriage which can be dissolved by consent or at the will of one of the parties should be recognised as a valid marriage in this country has given rise to some discussion in this country, especially in view of the Russian law which at one time seems to have allowed complete freedom of divorce, but it is probable that the mere fact that a foreign marriage can be brought to an end in such a way will not be regarded as contrary to English standards of morality.[40] It has not been shown that such freedom of divorce has necessarily led to a laxer standard of married life in those communities in which it is recognised.

The problem of morality also arises when a plaintiff seeks to enforce a foreign judgment in this country. It is established that if such a judgment has been obtained fraudulently it will not be enforced in this country, but this does not enable an unsuccessful party to allege that the foreign court was misled by perjured testimony. The English court is careful not

---

[38] [1946] P. 122.
[39] [1946] P. 27.
[40] *Har-Shefi* v. *Har-Shefi* [1953] 3 W.L.R. 200.

to retry a case decided by a foreign court. The most usual ground for holding a foreign judgment invalid is that it is contrary to natural justice, but exactly what is meant by natural justice it is difficult to say. Perhaps this has been best stated by Professor Cheshire when he says [41]: " Any impropriety in the foreign proceedings which has deprived a party of an opportunity to present his side of the case will be regarded as a violation of natural justice." [42]

ABUSE OF RIGHTS

Finally I must refer to the doctrine concerning the " abuse of legal rights " which has been much canvassed by Continental legal philosophers and has roused a certain amount of discussion in this country.[43] It has been argued that as the primary purpose of the law must be to do justice, it is wrong to ask the law to enforce a legal right in circumstances where such enforcement will lead to obvious injustice. There ought to be, according to this view, no absolute rights which are not subject to a higher equity. Many of the Continental codes have provisions giving effect to this doctrine, and, in spite of a certain amount of criticism, it seems to be generally accepted by Continental jurists as sound. It is difficult to determine, however, to what extent it has been used in practice, and to what degree it has proved satisfactory. It is clear that the English law has never adopted this

[41] p. 632.
[42] *Cf. Rudd* v. *Rudd* [1924] P. 72.
[43] Professor H. Gutteridge's article in (1933) 5 Cambridge L.J. 22 is of particular interest as he discusses the various Continental provisions on this subject.

principle. If a man possesses a legal right he is entitled to have that right enforced, however harsh the result may be. The House of Lords in the case of *Mayor of Bradford* v. *Pickles* [44] refused to consider the allegation that Mr. Pickles was acting in an unsocial manner in digging wells on his own land for the sole purpose of interfering with the reservoir belonging to the plaintiffs, because his wrongful motive could not affect the exercise of his legal rights. Again a man may enforce a contractual right at common law although it can be of no benefit to him and may bring disaster to the defendant. [45] Similarly he may deliberately collect a number of obligations which have been incurred by one man and then sue on them, so as to force him into bankruptcy. From the moral standpoint it is obviously wrong for a man to exercise a right merely for the purpose of injuring another, but the English law is prepared to risk a conflict with the moral law so as to attain what it regards as the greater advantage of certainty. It may also be said that it is morally desirable that every man should know exactly what his rights and duties are without subjecting them to the equitable opinion of another person, even if the other person is a judge.

[44] [1895] A.C. 587.
[45] Wills J. in *Allen* v. *Flood* [1898] A.C. 1, 46, said: " Any right given by contract may be exercised against the giver by the person to whom it is granted, no matter how wicked, cruel or mean the motive may be which determines the enforcement of the right. It is hardly too much to say that some of the most cruel things that come under the notice of a judge are mere exercises of a right given by contract."

It has been suggested that the two nuisance cases of *Christie* v. *Davey* [46] and *Hollywood Silver Fox Farm, Ltd.* v. *Emmett* [47] are an exception to the strict English principle, but this is based on a misunderstanding of the law of nuisance. The law of nuisance is not concerned with what one does on one's own land, except in so far as it may affect the land of a neighbour. In the *Hollywood Silver Fox Farm Case* the defendant deliberately fired a shot-gun on his own land so as to frighten and injure the foxes on the plaintiff's farm. The court held that as the defendant had intended to cause this injury he brought himself within the law of nuisance because it was unreasonable for him to pour this noise over his neighbour's land. He was not merely exercising a liberty on his own land: he was violating his neighbour's right not to be interfered with in an unreasonable manner. These nuisance cases do not therefore derogate from the strict English doctrine that if a man is given a right by the law he is entitled to use it as he sees fit.

It may be suggested here that the English doctrine finds some justification in the history of the " abuse of right " doctrine in the field of international law. There the exercise of the doctrine has itself constituted an abuse. It has been used by States to repudiate their treaty obligations on the ground that it would be an abuse of right for the other parties to ask for their enforcement. Combined with the doctrine of *rebus sic stantibus* it has sometimes tended to destroy the force of treaties that have been freely entered into

---

[46] [1893] 1 Ch. 316.
[47] [1936] 2 K.B. 468.

and solemnly recognised. Such a result can hardly be described as moral.

THE INFLUENCE OF LAW ON MORALS

So far I have been concerned with the influence of the moral law on English law. I must now say a few words concerning the contrary process in which we find that the law has gradually influenced the moral conceptions of the community. It is sometimes said that in the relationship between law and morals law must always be the laggard, and that it is only after the moral law has been long established that the law of the State succeeds in catching up with it. It is undoubtedly true that there are parts of the present law which express the moral convictions of the past rather than those of today, but it is equally true that there have been a number of instances in our history where the civil law has been in advance of the general moral law, and where it may be said that moral convictions have been altered under legal leadership. An obvious illustration of this can be found in the criminal law against duelling. It took generations of effort on the part of the judges who had to administer the law before the present moral conviction that duelling is wrongful was established. Today a man who becomes engaged in a duel would be regarded as a moral wrongdoer: two centuries ago a man who refused to accept a challenge might well have been regarded as a social outcast. Perhaps another illustration of the influence of law on morals can be found in the various Married Women's Property Acts. In his play *The Twelve-Pound Look* Sir James Barrie drew a picture which showed what economic independence might mean to a woman.   It cannot be doubted that the economic independence which women have achieved has in large part been a fundamental cause in altering the social and moral convictions and standards in this country in recent years.   The Acts which gave independence to married women resulted from the efforts of a limited group of persons, and could not have been said to represent the general moral convictions of the country.

We can see a similar influence on morality being exerted by the law of tort and by the criminal law. Without our realising it, we may find that what we have come to regard as a moral obligation really finds its origin in the law.   On this point Professor Fuller has said [48]:

" Actually, if we look to those rules of morality which have enough teeth in them to act as serious deterrents to men's pursuit of their selfish interests, we will find that far from being ' extra-legal ' they are intimately and organically connected with the functionings of the legal order.   I may think that I drive carefully because it is my moral duty to do so as a good citizen, and I may suppose that the law merely takes over my standard of driving—which is, of course, that of the prudent man—as a test to apply to drivers less virtuous than myself.   I forget to what extent my conceptions of my duty as a driver have been shaped by the daily activities of the traffic police."

[48] *The Law in Quest of Itself,* 1940, p. 136.

I have already referred to the close relationship between law and morality in the field of commerce and industry. The traffic here has not been all one way because in many instances it has been the law which has enabled the moral leaders of the commercial community to impose their high standards on some not over-enthusiastic followers. On this point that great commercial lawyer Lord Atkin said [49]:

" The law maintains and publicly maintains and enforces a very high standard of integrity. Law and morality are, of course, not synonymous, and the demands of morality and the moral code no doubt extend into spheres where the law does not set its foot. But in dealings as between man and man the English law does set up a high, but not too high, attainable standard of honesty and fair dealing which, to my mind, is of the very greatest value to the whole community and especially to the commercial community."

The instances which I have given—and there are many more which could have been added to the list— make it clear that the civil law has played an important part in shaping the moral law of this country. This is hardly surprising because both of them are essential and interrelated parts of our civilisation. Any attempt to separate them in action is to cut " the seamless web " of English law, as Maitland has called it, because the law is seamless not only in its history but also in the forces which give it its life.

[49] Presidential Address, 1930, the Holdsworth Club, Birmingham University.

CONCLUSION

In these lectures I have attempted to show that the essence of law does not lie either in the fact that it has been commanded by someone in authority or that it contains a sanction in case the rule is violated. It is, I believe, a rule of human conduct which is recognised as being obligatory. It is the sense of obligation which gives the rule its legal character. The relationship between law and morals is therefore of the utmost importance because the recognition that a rule is obligatory under the moral law will be a powerful element in producing a similar recognition concerning the obligatory nature of civil law.

When we turn to English civil law we find that the principles and rules of constitutional law are recognised as obligatory by both the representatives of the State who are in authority and by those who are subjects of the Crown. It is correct therefore to speak of the Constitution as a body of legal rules even though no one has commanded them and although there is no legal sanction attached to them. The relationship between this constitutional law and the moral law is two-fold. First, the recognition that it is a moral duty to obey the rules of the Constitution until they are altered in accordance with the proper procedure is one of the most powerful elements on which the recognition of the obligatory nature of the Constitution is based. Secondly, the principles of the Constitution are identical with the principles of the moral law as it is understood in the Western world. In contrast with this we can see that the weakness of international law is found in the lack of moral law, and not in the international machinery.

In the various branches of English law we have found that the relationship between civil law and moral law is a close one. Even in such subjects as the law of property and procedural law, which are regarded as peculiarly technical, the moral element is of great importance. Although few people would be prepared to argue that there are no parts of English law today which do not lag behind the generally recognised moral standards of the community, these " gaps " are comparatively rare and are of minor importance.

The conclusion which I have therefore reached is that the strength of English law, from the basic rules of the Constitution to a minor regulation issued by a local authority, depends in large part on the fact that the people of this country recognise that they are under an obligation to obey the law, and that this sense of obligation is based, not on force or fear, but on reason, morality, religion, and the inherited traditions of the nation. It is for this reason that we can truly say that the common law is our common heritage.